EMERIL LAGASS FRYER 360

THE FAMILY-APPROVED COOKBOOK:

150+ Tasty, New Orleans, Vegetarian, Gluten-Free, Kid-Friendly & More Recipes for Everyday

BY
JILLIAN LOVERTIME

© Copyright 2020 by - All rights reserved.

This document is geared towards providing exact and reliable information in regards to the topic and issue covered. The publication is sold with the idea that the publisher is not required to render accounting, officially permitted, or otherwise, qualified services. If advice is necessary, legal or professional, a practiced individual in the profession should be ordered.

- From a Declaration of Principles which was accepted and approved equally by a Committee of the American Bar Association and a Committee of Publishers and Associations.

In no way is it legal to reproduce, duplicate, or transmit any part of this document in either electronic means or in printed format. Recording of this publication is strictly prohibited and any storage of this document is not allowed unless with written permission from the publisher. All rights reserved.

The information provided herein is stated to be truthful and consistent, in that any liability, in terms of inattention or otherwise, by any usage or abuse of any policies, processes, or directions contained within is the solitary and utter responsibility of the recipient reader. Under no circumstances will any legal responsibility or blame be held against the publisher for any reparation, damages, or monetary loss due to the information herein, either directly or indirectly.

Respective authors own all copyrights not held by the publisher.

The information herein is offered for informational purposes solely, and is universal as so. The presentation of the information is without contract or any type of guarantee assurance.

The trademarks that are used are without any consent, and the publication of the trademark is without permission or backing by the trademark owner. All trademarks and brands within this book are for clarifying purposes only and are the owned by the owners themselves, not affiliated with this document.

Table of contents

Introduction: 7
Chapter 01: Understanding Air fryer 8
1.1 What is an Air fryer? 8
1.2 How to use an Air fryer? 9
1.3 Safety precautions for using an Air fryer 11
1.4 Cleaning of an Air fryer 13
Chapter 02: Starters and Breakfast 16
2.1 Omelette in Emeril Lagasse Power Air Fryer: 16
2.2 Dehydrated Oranges: 16
2.3 Seafood Tacos: 17
2.4 Wedged Potatoes: 19
2.5 BBQ Pulled Pork-Stuffed Corn Muffins: 19
2.6 Air Fried French toast: 20
2.7 Air Fried Cinnamon Rolls: 21
2.8 Air Fried Bagels: 21
2.9 Dehydrated Strawberries in the Power Air Fryer 360: 22
2.10 Air Fried Frozen Biscuit and Sausage Patty: 23
2.11 Air Fried Pillsbury Toaster Strudel: 24
2.12 Air Fried Frozen Hot Pocket: 24
2.13 Air Fried Baked Apple: 24
2.14 Air Fried Cranberry Pecan Muffins: 25
2.15 Air Fryer Cherry Turnovers: 26

2.16 Air Fried Bacon: 27
2.17 Air Fried Frittata: 27
2.18 Air Fried Egg and Bacon Bite Cups: 28
2.19 Air Fried Sausage: 29
2.20 Air Fried French toast Sticks: 29
2.21 Crispy Air Fried Sweet Potato Hash Browns: 30
2.22 Air Fried Roasted Potatoes: 31
2.23 Air Fried Loaded Hash Browns: ... 31
2.24 Air Fried Cinnamon Sugar Donuts: 32
2.25 Air Fried Sweet Potato Biscuits: 33
2.26 Air Fried Puffed Egg Tarts: 34
2.27 Air Fried Breakfast Pockets: 35
2.28 Air Fried Hard Boiled Eggs: 35
Chapter 03: Lunch 37
3.1 Air Fried Southwest-Style Pork Loin: 37
3.2 Meatball Pasta Bake: 38
3.3 Rosemary and Salt Roasted Shrimp with Garlic Butter Dipping Sauce: 39
3.4 Snapper Fillets Baked in a Creole Sauce: 40
3.5 Buttermilk Fried Chicken: 41
3.6 Asian Oven Baked Flounder: 42
3.7 Flank Steak: 43
3.8 Bacon and Corn Pudding: 44

3.9 New York-Style Thin Crust Pizza: ..46

3.10 Reuben Sandwich: 47

3.11 Roasted Garlic White Pizza with Garlic Sauce: 48

3.12 Roasted Salmon: 49

3.13 Blue Cheese-Stuffed Burgers: 50

3.14 Air Fried Citrus and Honey Glazed Ham: 51

3.15 Air Fried New York Strip Steak with Red Wine Sauce: 52

3.16 Air Fried Roasted Duck: 53

3.17 Grilled Chicken Breast Strips: 53

3.18 Air Fried St. Louis Spareribs: 54

3.19 Southern Fried Chicken: 55

3.20 Air Fried Roasted Broccoli: 56

3.21 Air Fried Panko Breaded Chicken Drumsticks: 56

3.22 Turkey and Hot Sausage Chili: 57

3.23 Juicy Air Fried Cheeseburgers: 58

3.24 Air Fried Bacon Grilled Cheese: 59

3.25 Air Fried Honey Glazed Ham: 59

3.26 Air Fried Juicy Cornish Hens: 60

3.27 Air Fried Beef Meatballs BBQ: 61

3.28 Air Fried Garlic Roasted Green Beans: 62

3.29 Air Fried Homemade Crispy French Fries: 62

3.30 Air Fried Crispy Fish Sandwich: ...63

3.31 Air Fried Buffalo Cauliflower: 64

3.32 Air Fryer Pepperoni Pizza: 65

3.33 Fried Shrimp Po' Boy Sandwich: ...65

3.34 Air Fried Parmesan Breaded Chicken Tenders: 66

3.35 Air Fried Mac and Cheese Balls: ...67

Chapter 04: Dinner 68

4.1 Air Fryer Paprika Chicken Wings: ..68

4.2 Spicy Buttermilk Fried Chicken with Pepper Jelly Drizzle: 68

4.3 Crispy Air-Fried Shrimp Sliders: 70

4.4 Rotisserie Chicken: 71

4.5 Southwest Cowboy Steak with Skillet Corn Sauce and Tortillas: 72

4.6 Crab Meat Imperial: 73

4.7 Giant Stuffed Burger: 74

4.8 Sunday Roast Beef with Gravy: 75

4.9 Baby Bam Burgers: 76

4.10 Pecan-Crusted Codfish: 77

4.11 Spicy Short Ribs Smothered with Red Gravy: 78

4. 12 Roasted Leg of Lamb: 79

4.13 Cornish Hens: 81

4.14 Emeril's Stuffed Shrimp: 81

4.15 Steak Roulade: 82

4.16 Bourbon Rotisserie Pork Roast: 83

4.17 Air Fried Chicken Breast: 84

4.18 Air Fried Crispy Balsamic Brussels sprouts: 85

4.19 Air Fried Marinated Steak: 86

4.20 Air Fried Cilantro Marinated Chicken Thighs: 87

4.21 Air Fried Beef Taco Egg Rolls: 88

4.22 Air Fried Catfish: 89

4.23 Air Fried Crab Cakes: 89

4.24 Air Fried Watchers Mozzarella Cheese Sticks: 90

4.25 Air Fried Crispy Fish Sandwich: ... 91

4.26 Air Fried Cheese and Chicken Quesadillas: 92

4.27 Air Fryer Crab Fried Rice: 93

4.28 Air Fried Fish Sticks: 94

4.29 Air Fried Thai Chili Chicken Wings: 94

4.30 Air Fryer Beef Empanadas: 95

4.31 Air Fried Corn Dogs: 97

4.32 Air Fryer Grilled Chicken Kebabs: 98

4.33 Crispy Air Fried Bang Bang Shrimp: 99

Chapter 05: Desserts and Breads 101

5.1 Brown Butter-Pecan Bread Pudding with Bourbon Sauce: 101

5.2 Cinco Leches Cake: 102

5.3 White Chocolate Macadamia Bread Pudding: 103

5.4 Lemon Poppyseed Cake: 105

5.5 Air Fried Peanut Butter and Jelly Doughnuts: 106

5.6 Air Fried Buttermilk Biscuits: 107

5.7 Scallion and Cheddar Biscuits: 108

5.8 Cheddar Jalapeño Cornbread: 109

5.9 Molten Chocolate Cakes: 110

5.10 Air Fried Garlic Bread: 112

5.11 Sweet Potato Pie in an Air Fryer: 112

5.12 Air Fryer Strawberry Pop-Tarts: . 114

5.13 Air Fryer Dessert Empanadas: 115

5.14 Air Fried Blueberry Muffins: 116

5.15 Air Fried Lemon Pound Cake: 117

5.16 Air Fried Chocolate Chip Cookies: 118

5.17 Paleo Pumpkin Air Fried Muffins: 119

Chapter 06: Snacks and Appetizers 121

6.1 Sicilian Style Air Fried Broccoli: 121

6.2 Blue Cheese-Stuffed Burgers: 122

6.3 Mac & Cheese: 123

6.4 Baked Mushrooms Stuffed With Crabmeat Imperial: 124

6.5 Gougeres Stuffed with Ham Mousse: 125

6.6 Garlicky Air Fried Shrimp: 126

6.7 Fried Green Beans with Garlic Lime Dip: 127

6.8 Korean Beef Wraps: 128

6.9 Wild Mushroom and Manchego Pizza: 128

6.10 Pecan Crusted Chicken: 130

6.11 Shrimp & Pork Vietnamese Egg Rolls: 131

6.12 Bacon Wrapped Asparagus: 132

6.13 Mini Pizzas with Hot Italian Sausage: 133

6.14 Kicked-Up Tuna Melts: 134

6.15 Dehydrated Onions: 134

6.16 Garlicky Air Fried Shrimp: 135
6.17 Air Fried Crispy Brussels sprouts with Lemon, Garlic, and Parmesan: 136
6.18 Air Fried Mini Corn dogs: 136
6.19 Air Fried Spaghetti Squash: 137
6.20 Frozen Air Fried Chicken Nuggets: 138
6.21 Air Fried Roasted Asparagus: 138
6.22 Air Fried Tortilla Chips: 139
6.23 Air Fried Zucchini Chips: 140
6.24 Air Fried Cream Cheese and Bacon Stuffed Jalapeno Poppers: 141
6.25 Air Fried Crispy Crab Rangoon: .. 141
6.26 Air Fried Pizza Rolls: 143
6.27 Air Fried Wontons: 144
6.28 Air Fried Tater Tots: 144
6.29 Air Fried Cheese Stuffed Mushrooms: 146
6.30 Air Fried Potato Wedges: 146
6.31 Air Fried Cheesy Garlic Bread: 147
6.32 Air Fried Crunchy Pickles: 148
6.33 Air Fried Cornbread: 149
6.34 Air Fried Croutons: 149
6.35 Air Fried Beef Jerky: 150
6.36 Crispy Air Fried Artichoke Hearts: 151
6.37 Ranch Seasoned Air Fryer Chickpeas: 151
Chapter 07: 30 Day Meal Plan 153
7.1 Week 1 153
7.2 Week 2 153
7.3 Week 3 154
7.4 Week 4 154
Conclusion: 156

Introduction:

The Emeril AirFryer 360 is a multi-cooker air fryer & countertop oven that enables air frying, roasting, rotisserie, slow cooking, baking, broiling, and more. You have all the comfort of a small countertop oven & much more. Its size which is XL allows you a cooking room that big families and parties need to have. Replace your toaster, air fryer, convection, pizza, broiler, roaster, slow cooker, dehydrator, and much more with the12 revolutionary Smart One-Touch Buttons. Air bake homemade cookies with chocolate chips, slow cook juicy ribs, fry French fries and healthy dehydrated snacks, etc. It does not need additional oil. The trick is Air Flow Technology of the Emeril AirFryer 360. Traditional convections have just 3 heating components, but your food cooks equally on the bottom, top, and sides with the five heating components and the Air Frying Fan of the Emeril AirFryer 360. Two separate cooking racks, for the purpose of air frying with less oil fried foods a high-sided netted Crisper Tray, and a special Pizza Rack for properly crisp crust are supplied with the Power AirFryer 360. You even get a separate Rotisserie Spit in your AirFryer 360, which helps you rotisserie turkey, roulades, chicken, and more. Plus, all crumbs from the food are caught by the Drip Tray, so cleaning it is so easy.

Crisp in a swirl of superheated hot air rather than fat and prepare your favorite recipes. Combined with 360 ° seamless airflow, intuitive heating helps minimize cooking time and also produces perfectly cooked with crispier results. This is known to be an oven alternative and the claim is impossible to disagree with. It has several features, is very big, and heats up to the maximum temperature of about 400 degrees almost instantly. From meat and vegetables to toast and even dehydrating, you can cook everything with our Emeril Lagasse Air Fryer 360. Food, roast, toast, broil, bake, toast bagels, dehydrate, rotisserie, prepare pizza, cook steadily, and warm food can be reheated. There are a number of features. Plus, with 5 heating elements, it does everything. For all your meals, this ensures rapid, even cooking. Whether you make chicken breast from an air fryer or whatever else, it cooks easily and deliciously.

Chapter 01: Understanding Air fryer

This chapter gives detail about the air fryers. What is an air fryer, which foods you can cook in an air fryer, and what are the health benefits of air fried food includes in the chapter? How an air fryer actually works and how you can look for the best fryer are also discussed in detail and depth. What are the safety hazards of an air fryer, how to reduce them, and how to deep clean your air fryer are also discussed?

1.1 What is an Air fryer?

Counter room in almost every kitchen is a hot item. It's easy to crowd and load with the new cooking equipment even though you have a ton of them. However, a fryer is something you will want to find room for. In the way that it roasts and bakes, an air fryer device is identical to an oven, but the distinction is that the heat providing units are placed only on top as well as being driven by a big strong fan, producing a portion of food that in no time is super crisp and most importantly, with little oil as compared to deep-fried equivalents. Usually, air fryers heat up very easily and, due to the union of a centralized source of heat and the fan placement and size and, they make meals uniformly and quickly.

The cleanup is another big part of the air frying operation. Many racks and baskets for air fryers are dishwasher protected. We recommend a decent dish brush, for those who are not really dishwasher friendly. Without making you crazy, it'll get deeply into all the crannies and nooks and that encourage air movement.

Things you can cook in an air fryer:

Air fryers are quick and can be used to cook all types of fresh food, such as chicken, fish, beef, pork chops, and vegetables, or heat frozen foods, once you learn how they work. Since they're still so juicy, most meats do not need additional oil, so just spice them with your favorite herbs and salt and spices. As fewer humidity results in crispier results, make sure you adhere to dry flavorings. Wait for the last few minutes of preparation whether you choose to baste the beef with honey or barbecue sauce.

Lean meat cuts, or items containing minimal or no fat, need browning and crisping with oil. Before seasoning, spray the pork chops and boneless meat breasts with a touch of butter. Due to the high smoke point, vegetable oil or canola oil is generally preferred, indicating it can handle high heat in the fryer.

Prior to air fried, vegetables still need to be fried a little in cooking oil. Before air-frying, we suggest splattering them by using salt, just use even less than you're used to. A ton of spices is filled with the dry, air fried pieces. We love Brussels sprouts, baby potato halves, and florets of broccoli, for air frying. They're so crispy coming out. It seems like sweet potatoes, beets, and butternut squash, are all becoming sweeter, and it doesn't take much time for green beans and peppers.

Knowing air fried food is healthy or not?

Air fried food has a close flavor and consistency to the performance of a deep-fried food. On the ground, crispy; on the inside, juicy. You do need to use a limited amount of oil though, or any at all depending upon what you are cooking. If you agree to use just 1 to 2 tbs of oil which is plant-based with flavoring, as well as you stick to air frying your vegetables rather than any other thing, air frying is certainly a better option as opposed to deep-frying. The secret to minimizing the likelihood of chronic illness, maintaining long-term wellness as we age, and weight maintenance, is any gadget that assists your family and you in your veggie game.

Some air-frying stuff might not be good for you, however. Air fried fish increased the quantity of a material named COPs cholesterol oxidation products in one analysis. COPs develop as, during frying, the cholesterol present in fish or meat breaks down. These compounds are related by studies to artery hardening, cancer, heart disease, and other illnesses. The study reveals that one approach to lower the number of COPs while you air-fried fish is to include fresh parsley, chives, or a combination of the two. To decrease these in air-fried foods, these herbs serve as antioxidants. It also suggests that air frying curbs the fatty acids named as omega-3 in seafood. Such good fats help to increase the amount of good Hydrochloric cholesterol and lower your blood pressure and can help protect your heart.

1.2 How to use an Air fryer?

Looking for the best Air fryer:

A number of various sizes and kinds of the air fryers are now accessible. Try the XXL Air Fryer of Philips, which will cook a whole chicken or 6 servings of fries if you're preparing for a party.

If there is a little counter space, consider the Philips Advance Air Fryer that circulates hot air using proprietary technology, delivering crunchy, satisfying performance. And with the same power and Turbo Star technology, this next-level air fryer has a more portable size, which ensures uniform cooking of food. Now without shame, you can eat all the food that is fried.

You may also obtain a number of different accessories, such as a grill pan, rack, pans, muffin, and mesh baskets for fun, to improve the universality of an air fryer even more.

Few important tips for of an Air fryer usage:

Following are some important tips for using an air fryer effectively:

1. Shake well:

Make sure that you open the air fryer and you shake your food around when it fries in the basket of the machine, compressing smaller items such as chips and French fries. Rotate them after 5-10mins with the better performance.

2. Spray on foods:

To make sure they don't cling to your basket and gently brush the foods with the cooking spray or apply little amount of oil.

3. Master your other cooking methods:

The air fryer is not only for frying, it is also useful for other healthier ways of cooking, such as baking, roasting, and grilling.

4. Avoid overcrowding of food:

Offer food plenty of room to allow the air to flow efficiently, which is what gives you crisp performance.

5. Keep your machine dry:

To avoid unnecessary smoke and splattering, pat your food dry before frying it, for instance, if they're marinated. Also, ensure that you empty the fat from bottom machine occasionally when you are preparing some high-fat items like chicken wings.

Working of an Air fryer:

Your fryer is almost like a wonderful convection oven. It's tiny but strong, and it can give you roasted, grilled, or broiled food. You're unable to fry deep in it. The heat increases, because the top rack has always been the hottest place in a normal oven, which contributes to inconsistent doneness. It's also why a number of recipes of cookies instruct you to switch baking sheets halfway through baking from back to front and top to bottom. However, fans blast hot air around a convection oven such that the heat is equalized in the oven. On the other hand, air fryers are not quite like condensation ovens, and their ventilation is designed to mimic the deep-frying heat delivery in hot fat more closely. But the oven technology is even strong enough for our purposes.

Few air fryer mistakes one can make:

It won't explode your face off to do any of the following stuff but aim to stop them.

Do not be totally freehanded with oil:

For the oil, use a light hand. Under the grating, an excess amount of oil accumulated in the drawer, so if there's too much storage, it may smoke. If the product already includes fat skin-on meat, for instance, or some frozen fried food, you do not have to oil the product at all. However, vegetables profit from a light oil coating, since it serves to make them healthy and brown.

Avoid using an oil having a low smoke point:

For air frying, olive oil isn't perfect since it has a low point of smoke. Not only can it burn at high-level temperatures, but also an odd aftertaste will also form. The way to go is peanut oil, vegetable or canola oil, as well as other strong smoke-point oils.

Avoid greasing the drawer while using cooking spray:

It seems like it will be a smart idea, but over time, the baskets of an air fryer have a non - stick coating, so the cooking spray will affect the finish. Instead of using cooking spray, roll the food in oil, you're actually already doing that in certain situations, or wipe it down with a paper towel soaked with oil. The aid of extra oil is not required for already fried frozen foods.

Avoid overcrowding the drawer:

Air fryers do not have a huge space with all the room that they occupy on an artifact. Don't fill the drawer with food for better performance. Adding another couple of shaved beets or potato sticks is so appealing, but if you operate in tiny quantities, you'll understand from practice that the product cooks up quickly and comes out crunchier.

Avoid pouring the hot contents directly into a bowl:

To bring the fried food out, use a spoon or tongs. Excess oil pools in the basket under the adjustable grate, because if you yank the basket out and place it on a platter, hence the oil will leak out with the grate. This will render you burn, leave a mess, and contribute to extra greasy food.

1.3 Safety precautions for using an Air fryer

Some hazards you should be aware of:

It can be a source of worry for any person to improperly use your air fryer. Nevertheless, if you are using it actually in accordance with the directions issued by the manufacturer, you can appreciate the many benefits it has to bring. Any of the advantages provide lifetime and reliable features, and your air fryer would also not decline over time. For all of the air fryer operators, air fryer precaution is advised so you can have a perfect cooking exposure.

Also, it is of the greatest significance to note that it is never appropriate to scrub or disinfect the electrical units of the equipment and the housing underwater. It can result in shocks and short circuits that, if the gadget is working, may be fatal. It is discouraged to cover the bowl with oil. The machine is supposed to run without oil. It will create fire risks that might destroy the gadget and place you in dangerous situations by utilizing more than just the necessary amount of oil.

Users are often stopped when it is turned on from contacting the appliance. Since the air fryer is intended to be customer-friendly, consumers are cautioned to minimize distractions during action in order to avoid any risk of burns or shocks attributable to breakdowns. You can wait at least 25 minutes to be certain it has cooled off until you can begin cleaning your air fryer. It is strongly discouraged to contact the interior of the equipment during this period.

Most notably, you can hold kids and livestock safe from the machinery. Although the system is shock resistant, it still can be unsafe for children and livestock. Covering the appliance's outlet and inlets may have devastating consequences. The consistency of the product being cooked would be compromised because as there is no means for the air to reach or leave the device, it will create a major catastrophe that may lead to significant damage.

Precautionary measures to ensure the safety of an Air fryer:

Using any device can raise possible threats that can be minimized by implementing such protective steps. This will prove to be extremely successful in minimizing the likelihood of potential untoward events. These prevention strategies will do a lot of good, as simple as they can sound, and are relevant to nearly all of the equipment you have in the house and use on a daily basis.

You can determine the volt that is needed by the device before the use of it. If that is taken care of, to maintain consistency, you should equate it to the fixtures in your house. The power cords must be held away from the hot surfaces. The cords can be affected by extreme heat. It is strongly advisable to study the manual in order to gain an idea of the device. You should never, except if recommended by the maker, use the device for some other function.

Never left your device unattended. You will guarantee in this way, that everything is out of the control of your children and pets in this manner. There is never something you can put on top of the device. It is completely discouraged to use the fryer with damp hands. The need to do so is explanatory. It is safer to stop employing illegal workers or sending the fryer to the service facility if the fryer is really in need of maintenance. You should take full advantage of the warranty to request the producer to either fix the faulty product or substitute it. If your warranty has ended, to guarantee you have the absolute best fix, you should take your fryer to an approved service center. In the event of an emergency, you should still ask the manufacturer to suggest a suitable repairing service solution.

To avoid any crashes or leaks, it is strongly advisable for all consumers to position the device on a uniform and secure surface. You have to look out for super-hot steam when extracting your pan from the device. Since these machines are meant for domestic use, using them in some other setting is entirely wrong. If you properly hold an air fryer, there is a reduced chance of injury. It is recommended that you'll have to maintain it and disinfect it on daily basis, despite the reality that you're going to prepare meals in the device. As difficult as it might seem, it is very easy to maintain an air fryer.

It is reasonably easy to clean the basket and the pan with the critical part.

However, as it reduces the performance of the device and ultimately contributes to its loss due to short circuits and rust, it is important for you to stop washing the inner parts with water. Even before contemplating buying a single for your house, you should have a piece of good knowledge about how to operate the fryer. More specifically, you must determine whether or not you do require an air fryer.

It might fail if you buy one and it sits idle for so many months at one time, contributing to security risks. In addition, whenever it comes to storing and utilizing your fryer, you can also make sure you are not careless. The easiest approach to do this is to check the instructions given by the maker to make sure that your air fryer is used correctly. You would be able to defend yourself and escape any unexpected situations by bearing these considerations in mind.

1.4 Cleaning of an Air fryer

If you have already put your air fryer to use, you realize that you can always enjoy all your favorite fried foods with far less calories and less fat, with these trendy kitchenwares. But after that, you're actually frying, which ensures that you will have more grease to work with afterward. Since it's an air fryer, you're going to get a lot less quantity of greasy residue to wipe than utilizing a deep fryer. Know how to use things that you actually already have on hand to disinfect your air fryer.

Tips for the cleaning of an Air fryer:

Know the don'ts and do's of air fryer repair before you thoroughly clean your air fryer.

- To clear food remains and contaminants from your air fryer, do not use metal utensils, abrasive sponges, or steel wire brushes. The non-stick layer on your air fryer may be harmed by this.

- You should place half a lemon in the fryer's basket if you detect a foul odor coming from the air fryer and let it rest until cleaning for around 30 minutes.

- Do not dip your fryer in water. An electric gadget is a key device, so this would kill it.

Tips for deep cleaning of an Air fryer:

Read on for our directions on how to disinfect an air fryer deeply, whether it's been a while since you gave your fryer a thorough clean, or if you just don't know from where to start. This is what you're going to need:

- Damp cloth with microfiber or sponge that is non-abrasive
- Clean, dry cloth
- Baking Soda
- Dish cleaner
- Brush with soft-bristle scrub

Directions for cleaning process:

Initiate by unplugging the air fryer. Enable it for around 30 minutes to cool.

Remove the pans and baskets and clean with soapy hot water. Enable the pieces to be washed in hot soapy form of water for at least 8-10 mins before cleaning with a sponge which is non-abrasive if some of the parts have been baked with food or grease. Some of the components might be safe for dishwashing, but if you decide to use a dishwasher for washing, refer to the manual.

To clean the interior off, use a sponge which is a non-abrasive or wet microfiber cloth with a touch of dish soap. Wipe the soap away with a damp, clean towel.

Switch the device upside down and clean down the heating part using a moist cloth or sponge.

If the key device has some baked or rough remains, produce a paste using baking soda and water. And use a soft-bristle brush, scrub the paste onto the excess and wash away with a clean towel.

Wipe the outside with a wet cloth. With a clean, moist towel, wash away the soap.

Until re-assembling, dry all removable sections and the main device.

When you should clean your Air fryer?

After every single use:

Wash the pan, tray, and basket with hot water and soap any time when you use the fryer, or put these in the dishwasher. To make sure certain components are secure for dishwashing, take reference from the user's guide. You can also use a bit of liquid soap and a wet cloth over the region to disinfect the inner part easily. Rinse all the components and assemble them again.

Although these measures should not need to be taken after each use, cleaning these components will keep the air fryer running efficiently on occasion. To clean down the outer part every once and a while use a damp towel. You can also look for the residue or oil on the heating coil. Let the device cool then clean it with a moist cloth if you see anything there.

Chapter 02: Starters and Breakfast

This chapter will help you to learn and experiment with the different basic varieties of recipes that are used on daily basis in the breakfast timing or as starters regarding air fried recipes of an air fryer. It definitely consists of an infinite number of options to try according to your flavor.

2.1 Omelette in Emeril Lagasse Power Air Fryer:

Yield: 3-4

Cooking time: 8 min

Ingredients:

- 6 Large Eggs
- 2 Slices of Havarti Cheese
- Salsa
- 3 Chicken Tenderloins
- 1 Ounce Butter
- Sour Cream

Instructions:

Blend the eggs.

Place a pizza pan on the Emeril Lagasse Power Air Fryer 360 XL on the lowest stack level.

Coat with the butter a black 9" circular baking pan.

Set the Emeril Lagasse Power Air Fryer 360 XL to 350 ° F. Roast. Cook for 8 minutes.

To start pre-heating, press start.

The eggs are added to the plate.

Put the pan on the rack after pre-heat is completed.

Pause after 4 minutes and rotate the pan.

Then add the chicken to the side that has been cooked, then add some cheese.

For about last 4 minutes, cook the omelet.

Fold the omelet.

Top it with sour cream and salsa and eat it.

Nutrients:

Amount per 100 grams

Calories 154

Proteins 11g

Cholesterol 313mg

Carbohydrates 0.6g

Total fats 12g

2.2 Dehydrated Oranges:

Yield: Serves 10 to 12

Cooking time: 12 hours

Ingredients:

2 oranges, sliced 1/4 inch thick

Instructions:

Slide your Crisper Tray into Spot 2 on the Rack. Slide your Pizza Rack into Spot 5 on the Shelf. On the Pizza Rack and Crisper Tray, place the slices of oranges in place.

Rotate the Dehydrate configuration (120 degrees F) of the Program Selection Knob. Switch the Time Control Button on for 12 hours. To begin cooking period, click the Start or Pause Button. Cook until they're crisp.

Nutrients:

Amount per serving 40g

Calories 130

Carbohydrates 30g

Fats 0g

Protein 2g

Sodium 10mg

2.3 Seafood Tacos:

Cooking time: 18 mins

Yield: 10 Servings

Ingredients:

- 2 8-oz bags mesquite barbecue potato chips
- 4 Eggs
- 1 cup flour
- 0.25 cup buttermilk
- 16–20 shrimp, deveined, peeled & tails removed
- 2-pound flounder pieces
- Kernels of 2 ears corn
- 6 jalapeños, diced and seeded
- 1 pound tomatoes, diced
- 0.5 Red Onion, Diced
- Juice of 1 lime
- 0.5 orange pepper, diced
- 1 teaspoon Chili powder

- 0.25 ground cayenne pepper
- 0.5 teaspoon ancho chili powder
- 0.125 teaspoon cumin
- 0.5 cup sour cream
- 0.5 cup grapeseed oil
- 6 serrano peppers, minced and seeded
- 1 tablespoon fresh lime juice
- 2 tablespoon chopped cilantro leaves
- 0.125 teaspoon salt
- 20 6-in. flour tortillas
- 2 limes, wedged
- 0.125 teaspoon ground black pepper
- 3 avocados which are sliced

Instructions:

Crush your barbeque chips using a food processor.

To a small baking dish, add the flour.

Use a second dish to add the buttermilk and eggs and beat your eggs with a fork.

On a third platter, add your crushed chips.

In the flour, dredge the shrimp and flounder, then the mixture of eggs, and then the chips.

Slide your Crisper Tray into Spot 2 on the Rack. Place the Crisper Tray with the shrimp and flounder.

Choose the setting for Air fry (400 ° F/205 ° C for 18 minutes).). To begin cooking period, click the Start Button.

Mix the corn kernels, jalapeños, tomatoes, red onion, lime juice, orange pepper, curry powder, ancho chili powder, chili powder, cayenne pepper, grapeseed oil, and cumin in a bowl to create the tomato and corn salsa when the fish and shrimp are cooked.

In a separate dish, add the sour cream, cilantro leaves, serrano peppers, fresh lime juice, black pepper, and salt to create the serrano cream.

Remove the shrimp and fried fish from your Crisper Tray before the cooking time runs out and eat them with the tomato salsa and corn, serrano crema, and avocado slices on the tortillas. With the lime wedges, serve.

Nutrients:

Amount per serving

Calories 290

Protein 27.3g

Cholesterol 59.4mg

Fats 10.5g

Carbohydrates 23.2g

2.4 Wedged Potatoes:

Cooking time: 18mins

Yield: 6 Servings

Ingredients:

- 2 tablespoon Emeril's Essence Seasoning
- 2 tablespoon olive oil
- 4 russet potatoes, wedged and washed

Instructions:

In the olive oil, toss the potato wedges and brush with the Emeril's Essence Seasoning.

Slide your Crisper Tray into Position 2 on the Shelf. Place the Crisper Tray with half of the potatoes.

Rotate Program Selection Knob to the Air Fry setting (400 ° F/205 ° C for 18 mins.). To begin the cooking period, click the Start or Pause Button.

Take out the potatoes from your Crisper Tray as the timer hits 0. For the next batch of potatoes, repeat the cooking process. Serve with the steak.

Nutrients:

Amount per 100g

Calories 123

Fat 2.2g

Cholesterol 0g

Carbohydrates 26g

Protein 2.7g

2.5 BBQ Pulled Pork-Stuffed Corn Muffins:

Cooking time: 20mins

Yield: 6 Servings

Ingredients:

- 2 tablespoon butter, cooled and melted
- 0.75 cornmeal
- 2 cup all-purpose flour
- 0.33 cup sugar, plus more for sprinkling
- 0.75 teaspoon salt
- 1 tablespoon plus 1 tsp. baking powder
- 3 Eggs
- 0.5 cup of water
- 0.5 cup vegetable oil

- 2 tablespoon buttermilk
- 0.25 cup Barbeque sauce
- 0.25 cup Honey
- 2 tablespoon Heavy Cream
- 1.5 cup pulled pork

Instructions:

Butter the 6-cup, 7-oz muffin tray.

In a bowl, combine the flour, sugar, baking powder, cornmeal, and salt together.

In a separate bowl, combine the eggs, buttermilk, water, vegetable oil, cream, and honey together.

To finish the corn muffin mix, apply the wet ingredients to dry ingredients, and mix.

Combine the barbeque sauce and pulled pork.

Spoon the 2 tablespoon corn muffin mix into every muffin cup. Top your mix with 3 tablespoons pulled pork and then another 2 tablespoon corn muffin mix.

Slide your Pizza Rack into Shelf position no. 6.

Rotate the program selection knob to bake setting (325° F/165° C). Turn the Time Control Knob to 20 minutes. To begin the cooking period, click the Start/Pause Button. Place the muffin tray on the Pizza Rack when the Power Air Fryer 360 beeps to show it's preheated.

Remove the muffin tray once the timer hits 0. Prior to serving, let the muffins cool.

Nutrients:

Amount per serving

Calories 232kcl

Carbohydrates 22.7g

Cholesterol 52mg

Protein 11.5g

Fat 10.2g

2.6 Air Fried French toast:

Cooking time: 9 mins

Yield: 2 servings

Ingredients:

- 1/2 cup milk
- 1 tsp cinnamon
- 2 eggs
- Maple syrup
- 1/2 tbsp powdered sugar
- 4 slices bread
- 1/4 tsp vanilla extract

Instructions:

Preheat the power air fryer 360 for about 5 minutes to 176 ° C.

In a dish, mix the milk, cinnamon, and eggs with the butter. With a spoon, stir the blend until well combined.

In the egg better, dip your bread slice.

Before placing each one bread slice, place the baking paper in your air fryer.

In a layer, fry at 165 ° C for about 6 minutes, rotating the toast partly through frying for 3 minutes.

From your air fryer, extract the French toast that is freshly fried.

Place the toast on the plate. Sprinkle on top, sugar powder and, if needed, apply maple syrup.

Nutrients:

Amount per serving

Calories: 300 kcal

Fat 4g

Protein 4g

Carbs 6g

2.7 Air Fried Cinnamon Rolls:

Cooking time: 15 mins

Yield: 4 servings

Ingredients:

- 1 non-stick cooking spray
- 1 can cinnamon rolls

Instructions:

Using non-stick spray for cooking or baking paper rounds, put your cinnamon rolls in your power air fryer 360's basket.

Cook for 12-15 minutes at 171°C, rotating once.

Plate, top with icing, and then serve.

Nutrients:

Amount per serving

Calories: 52kcl

Fat: 3g

Carbohydrates: 6g

Protein: 0g

2.8 Air Fried Bagels:

Cooking time: 4 mins

Yield: 2 servings

Ingredients:

- 2 bagels at room temp or refrigerated, opened for toasting

Instructions:

Already heat the Emeril Lagasse air fryer for about 5 minutes to 176 ° C.

As if you want the toasted bagel inside, open the bagel. And if you want to make the inward smoother, keep it closed.

Add in bagels while keeping one layer to an air fryer.

Air-fry the bagels at 176° C temperature for about 4 minutes. Based on the personal toasting needs, you might want to extend 1 to 2 minutes if you do have bigger bagels.

Place jelly or cream cheese on top, and eat it.

Nutrients:

Amount per serving

Calories: 169kcl

Carbohydrates: 28g

Fat: 2g

Protein: 11g

2.9 Dehydrated Strawberries in the Power Air Fryer 360:

Cooking time: 3 hours

Yield: 10- 12 servings

Ingredients:

- 6 Strawberries, thinly sliced

Instructions:

Place your Crisper Tray with the strawberries which are sliced thinly.

Place your tray on the level of Dehydrate, 3rd from the lowest level.

To dehydrate, switch the option dial.

Adjust the level of temperature to 125 degrees F.

Switch your time dial down to three hours.

Click the button to start.

Enable the period for dehydration to finish and then enjoy the food.

Nutrients:

Amount per serving

Calories: 38kcl

Carbohydrates: 9g

Fat: 1g

Protein: 1g

2.10 Air Fried Frozen Biscuit and Sausage Patty:

Cooking time: 17-20 minutes

Yield: 6 servings

Ingredients:

- Sausage Patties, frozen
- Frozen Biscuits

Instructions:

To bake, switch the option dial.

Place the rack in your Power Air Fryer 360 at the place of Pizza, the second up from lowest position.

Adjust the temperature to 400 degrees F.

Switch to 17 minutes on the Time Dial.

Click the button to start.

The pre-heating of the Air Fryer 360 will start.

Place the sausage patties and biscuits on your Crisper Tray during pre-heating and wait for pre-heating to finish before placing it in the Air Fryer 360.

Click the Start button when pre-heating is finished. Switchback the timer to a complete 17 minutes, then.

To collect the drippings, put your baking pan on your pizza rack.

Position the tray in the Air Fryer 360 on the Air Fry rack level. This is just above the level of Pizza Rack.

Close and click the Start button on the Air Fryer 360. The cook will begin.

Enable 14 minutes to cook, then click the pause button to avoid cooking. Get the biscuits removed.

To resume cooking your sausage patties, click the Start button again.

Give time for the cooking to end.

The temperature of the meat is at least 170 ° F.

Nutrients:

Amount per serving

Calories 145

Carbohydrates 0.7g

Protein 14.1g

Fat 9g

2.11 Air Fried Pillsbury Toaster Strudel:

Cooking time: 5-7 minutes

Yield: 1-2 servings

Ingredients:

- Pillsbury Toaster Strudel, take frozen up to 6 hours

Instructions:

Switch to Toast on the option dial.

Move your Slices dial according to your number of waffles.

Turn your Darkness dial to a single less than, or of your choice, to the setting darkest. Please remember, more would be fried by those in front than by those in the rear.

Click the button to start.

Enable cooking for about 5-7 minutes and if you like a more consistent cook in general, you should rotate them halfway.

Nutrients:

Amount per serving

Calories 350

Fat 13g

Carbohydrates 53g

Protein 5g

2.12 Air Fried Frozen Hot Pocket:

Cooking time: 10 minutes

Yield: 2-3 servings

Ingredients:

- 2 to 3 Hot Pockets, frozen

Instructions:

Switch to bake on the option dial.

Place your Hot Pockets on the tray in the Air Fryer 360, on the third from the bottom rack level.

Turn the dial to a temperature of 450° F.

Switch to 10 minutes on the Time Dial.

Click the button to start.

During pre-heating, the Air Fryer 360 must begin to cook as well as pre-heat.

Enable the cook to finish and serve it.

Nutrients:

Amount per serving

Calories: 310kcal

Protein: 10g

Carbohydrates: 35g

Fat: 14g

2.13 Air Fried Baked Apple:

Cooking time: 20 minutes

Yield: 2 servings

Ingredients:

- 2 Tbsp. walnuts, chopped
- 1 medium pear or apple
- 2 Tbsp. raisins
- ¼ tsp. cinnamon
- ¼ cup of water
- 1 ½ tsp. light melted margarine
- ¼ tsp. nutmeg

Instructions:

Preheat the power fryer 360 to 350 degrees F.

Slice the pear or apple from the center in half and spoon some of the pulp out.

Place the pear or apple on the base of the power air fryer 360 or in the frying pan which must be equipped with an air fryer.

Combine the cinnamon, margarine, nutmeg, raisins, and walnuts in a shallow dish.

Spoon the pear or apple halves into the centers with this mixture.

Into the pan, add water.

Bake in the power air fryer for about 20 minutes.

Nutrients:

Amount per serving

Calories: 247kcl

Fat: 9g

Protein: 3g

Carbohydrates: 43g

2.14 Air Fried Cranberry Pecan Muffins:

Cooking time: 15 minutes

Yield: 6-8 muffins

Ingredients:

2 large eggs

1/4 cup cashew milk

1/2 tsp. vanilla extract

1/4 cup Monk fruit or you can also use any sweetener

1 1/2 cups Almond Flour

1 tsp. baking powder

1/4 cup pecans, chopped

1/8 tsp. salt

1/2 cup cranberries

1/4 tsp. cinnamon

Instructions:

Add the milk, vanilla essence, and eggs to the blender and mix for 20-30 seconds.

Include the flour of almond, baking powder, sugar, salt, and cinnamon and mix for another time of 30-45 seconds until well mixed.

The blender container is separated from the foundation and 1/2 of the fresh pecans and cranberries are blended in. Fill silicone cups with the mixture. Use the remaining fresh cranberries for topping each of the muffins.

Place your muffins in the basket of the air fryer and bake for about 12-15 minutes on 325 or until the cake tester comes out totally clean.

Remove from the fryer and refrigerate on the wire tray.

Drizzle some of your muffins with a syrup glaze or molten white chocolate if needed.

Nutrients:

Amount per serving

Calories 136kcl

Carbohydrates 20.4g

Protein 2.3g

Fat 5.2g

2.15 Air Fryer Cherry Turnovers:

Cooking time: 25 minutes

Yield: 8 turnovers

Ingredients:

- 10 oz can, cherry pie filling
- 17 oz package puff pastry, 4 sheets
- 1 beaten egg
- Cooking oil
- 2 tablespoons of water

Instructions:

On a smooth surface, lay the sheets of pastry.

Unfold all sheets of pastry dough. Slice per sheet into four squares, creating a total of 8 squares.

To make an egg wash, beat your egg in a small container together with the water.

To spray across the edges of every square with the mixture of egg, use your fingertips or a brush used for cooking.

Fill the center of every square sheet with 1 to 1 1/2 tbsp of pie cherry filling. Do not stuff the pastry with overfill.

To build a triangle as well as seal the dough, fold your dough across diagonally. To seal, use the backside of a fork to push lines onto each turnover's open edges.

To release the turnovers, make 3 slits within the top of its crust.

With the egg mixture, paste the top of every turnover.

With cooking oil, spray the basket of Emeril Lagasse power air fryer 360 and insert the turnovers. And make sure that they do not hit the turnovers and do not pile them. If required, cook in batches.

Fry for 8 minutes at 370 degrees.

Before removing from the power air fryer, permit your pastries to cool down for about 2-3 minutes. This will guarantee that they don't stick.

Nutrients:

Amount per serving

Calories: 224kcal

Protein: 4g

Carbohydrates: 27g

Fat: 12g

2.16 Air Fried Bacon:

Cooking time: 11 minutes

Yield: 11 slices

Ingredients:

- 11 slices of bacon, take any

Instructions:

Divide the bacon in two, then put it in the Emeril Lagasse air fryer 360 for the first half.

Adjust the temperature to 400 degrees Celsius and set the timer for 10 minutes.

To see if anything has to be rearranged, search it halfway through and tongs are helpful in this.

You will cook for the remaining time. Check for the doneness needed.

Nutrients:

Amount per Serving

Calories 91 kcal

Fat 8g

Cholesterol 14mg

Protein 2g

2.17 Air Fried Frittata:

Cooking time: 20 mins

Yield: 2 servings

Ingredients:

- 4 lightly beaten eggs
- ¼ pound sausage for breakfast, crumbled and fully cooked
- Cooking spray
- ½ cup shredded Cheddar cheese or Monterey Jack cheese blend
- 1 green chopped onion
- 2 tablespoons diced bell red pepper
- 1 pinch of cayenne pepper

Instructions:

In a dish, combine the eggs, sausage, Cheddar cheese, onion, bell pepper, and cayenne and blend them.

The air fryer should be preheated to 180 degrees C. Spray with the help of cooking spray on a nonstick cake pan.

Add the mixture of eggs to the prepared tray of cake.

Cook in a power air fryer for about 18 to 20 minutes until the frittata is set.

Nutrients:

Amount per Serving

Calories: 380 kcal

Protein: 31.2g

Fat: 27.4g

Carbohydrates: 2.9g

2.18 Air Fried Egg and Bacon Bite Cups:

Cooking time: 25 mins

Yield: 8 servings

Ingredients:

- 6 large eggs
- Pepper and salt to taste
- 2 tablespoons of milk or heavy whipping cream
- ¼ cup chopped green peppers
- ¼ cup onions, chopped
- ¼ cup chopped red peppers
- ¼ cup fresh spinach, chopped
- ¼ cup mozzarella cheese, shredded
- ½ cup shredded cheddar cheese
- 3 slices of crumbled and cooked bacon

Instructions:

Add the eggs to a big sized mixing bowl.

Then add in the pepper, cream, and salt to taste. Stir to combine them.

Spray in the red peppers, green peppers, onions, cheeses, spinach, and bacon. Add only half of your ingredients here. Stir to integrate well together.

Insert the silicone cups in the power air fryer before putting in the egg better. This way you do not have to move your filled cups.

Put the mixture of eggs into each one of the silicone cups. Use your cooking spray initially.

Then sprinkle the half remaining portion of all of the vegetables.

Cook your egg bites cups for about 12-15 mins at 300 degrees. You can check the center of one with the help of a cake tester. The eggs have set, when the cake tester comes out clean.

Nutrients:

Amount per serving

Calories: 119 kcal

Fats: 9g

Proteins: 8g

Carbohydrates: 2g

2.19 Air Fried Sausage:

Cooking time: 20 minutes

Yield: 5 servings

Ingredients:

- 5 uncooked or raw sausage

Instructions:

Line the basket of the air fryer with baking paper. The grease would be taken up by baking paper to keep the power air fryer 360 from burning. Place your sausage on the top of the paper. It is okay to touch the sausages.

Cook at 360 degrees for about 15 minutes. Open and flip it then cook for an extra 5 mins or until the core temperature of the sausage exceeds 160 degrees. You can use a thermometer for meat. You should flip partly through as well. Before serving, let it cool.

Nutrients:

Amount per serving

Calories: 260kcal

Carbohydrates: 3g

Fats: 21g

Proteins: 14g

2.20 Air Fried French toast Sticks:

Cooking time: 22 minutes

Yield: 12 sticks

Ingredients:

- 1 tablespoon melted butter, measured in a solid-state
- 4 slices Texas Toast bread
- 1 teaspoon vanilla
- 1 beaten egg
- 1 teaspoon ground cinnamon
- 2 tablespoons sweetener
- 1/4 cup milk

Instructions:

Every piece of bread is sliced into 3 strips. With the melting butter, add in the sweetener, beaten egg, cinnamon, vanilla, and milk, to the dish. Stir to blend.

Use a cooking oil spray to spray your air fryer's basket.

In the better of French toast, dredge every slice of bread. Be cautious not to dredge too much into the batter with each stick. If so, you may sprint away from the batter.

Place the sticks of French toast in the basket of an air fryer 360. Don't get overcrowded.

Use cooking oil to spray.

Air Fried it at 370 degrees for about 8 minutes.

Open your power fryer and turn the French toast. Cook for about 2-4 more minutes or until it gets crisp.

Nutrients:

Amount per serving

Calories: 52kcal

Carbohydrates: 7g

Fat: 2g

Protein: 2g

2.21 Crispy Air Fried Sweet Potato Hash Browns:

Cooking time: 50 minutes

Yield: 4 servings

Ingredients:

- 4 sweet potatoes peeled
- 1 teaspoon cinnamon
- 2 minced garlic cloves
- 1 teaspoon paprika
- 2 teaspoons olive oil
- Pepper and salt to taste

Instructions:

The larger holes of a grater are used to grind the potatoes.

In a bowl full of cold water, put your sweet potatoes. Enable 20-25 minutes for the potatoes to let them soak. To extract starch component from the sweet potatoes, soaking your potatoes in cold water may aid. This makes the potatoes crunchy.

Pour the water onto the potatoes and use a paper towel to dry them fully.

In a dry container, put the potatoes. Insert the garlic, olive oil, paprika, and, to taste, pepper, and salt. To mix the ingredients, whisk them well.

Take the power air fryer 360 and add in the potatoes.

Then cook at 400 degrees for ten minutes.

Open the fryer and shake up the potatoes. For an extra ten minutes, you can also cook.

Before serving, let it cool.

Nutrients:

Amount per serving

Calories: 134kcal

Carbohydrates: 32g

Fat: 2g

Protein: 4g

2.22 Air Fried Roasted Potatoes:

Cooking time: 25 minutes

Yield: 4 servings

Ingredients:

- 2 russet potatoes, sliced
- 2 sprigs fresh rosemary
- 1 teaspoon olive oil
- 2 garlic cloves, minced
- Pepper and salt to taste
- 1/2 teaspoon onion powder
- Cooking oil

Instructions:

Drizzle by using the olive oil on the potatoes and season to taste with the onion powder, garlic, pepper, and salt.

Spray a basket of power air fryer 360 with cooking oil.

Together with the thyme, add the potatoes to the power air fryer's basket. And do not overfill your basket. If required, cook in batches.

Air fry at 400 degrees for about 10 minutes.

Open and shake the air fryer's basket. Air fried until the potatoes are crispy on the exterior for an extra 2-7 minutes and soft to touch when penetrated with a fork.

Nutrients:

Amount per serving

Calories: 68kcal

Carbohydrates: 13g

Fat: 1g

Protein: 2g

2.23 Air Fried Loaded Hash Browns:

Cooking time: 45 minutes

Yield: 4 servings

Ingredients:

- 1/4 cup green peppers, chopped
- 3 russet potatoes
- 1/4 cup red peppers, chopped
- 2 garlic cloves chopped
- 1/4 cup chopped onions
- 1 teaspoon paprika
- 2 teaspoons olive oil
- Pepper and salt to taste

Instructions:

The larger holes of a grater are used to grate the potatoes.

Take a bowl of cool water and add in the potatoes. Enable 20-25 minutes for your potatoes to soak. To extract the starch component from the taken potatoes, soaking them in cold water will aid. This makes the potatoes crunchy.

Then pour the water on the potatoes and use a paper towel to dry them fully.

In a dry dish, put the potatoes. Insert the ginger, olive oil, salt, paprika, and pepper. To mix the ingredients, whisk well.

Use the air fryer and include the potatoes in it.

Cook at 400 degrees for ten minutes.

Open the fryer and shake up the potatoes. Add the peppers and onions that have been sliced. For an extra ten minutes, can also cook.

Nutrients:

Amount per serving

Calories: 246kcal

Carbohydrates: 42g

Fat: 3g

Protein: 6g

2.24 Air Fried Cinnamon Sugar Donuts:

Cooking time: 20 minutes

Yield: 8 servings

Ingredients:

- 1 teaspoon ground cinnamon
- Cooking oil spray
- 8 oz can of biscuits

- 1-2 teaspoons stevia, can also use 1/4 cup of table sugar instead

Instructions:

On a flat board, lay some biscuits. To make holes in the center of your biscuits, use a little biscuit cutter or a round cookie cutter.

Spray a basket of Emeril Lagasse air fryer with oil.

In an air fryer, put your donuts. Spray oil on the donuts. Don't have the donuts stacked. If required, cook in two phases.

Cook at 360 degrees for 4 minutes.

Open the fryer and then flip your donuts. For an extra 4 minutes, can also cook.

For the left donuts, repeat the process.

Spritz extra oil on the donuts.

In a separate dish, insert the sugar and cinnamon.

Coat the sugar and cinnamon onto the donuts.

Nutrients:

Amount per serving

Calories: 186kcal

Carbohydrates: 25g

Fat: 9g

Protein: 3g

2.25 Air Fried Sweet Potato Biscuits:

Cooking time: 35 minutes

Yield: 8 biscuits

Ingredients:

- 2 cups all-purpose flour
- 1/2 teaspoon salt
- 1/2 tablespoon baking powder
- 2 tablespoons sugar or sweetener
- 2 tablespoons cold unsalted butter
- 1 teaspoon cinnamon
- 1/4 cup plain non-fat Greek yogurt
- 1 egg
- 1/2 cup cooked mashed sweet potato, chilled
- 1 tablespoon water
- 4 teaspoons butter
- Optional Honey Butter
- 1 1/2 teaspoons honey

Instructions:

In a dish, combine the baking powder, flour, sweetener, cinnamon, and salt. Include mashed potatoes, yogurt, and butter.

To whisk, use a fork. Do not over-blend. Take the fork all the way into the blend and moisten the butter on the whole.

On a floured board, spread your dough out. To roll the dough in size 7 x 7 and 1/2 inches in height, use a pin or your hands. Don't make the dough overwork.

To cut your biscuits, cut them in any way you wish, use a cookie-cutter.

In a shallow container, beat the egg and mix it with some water and then stir. Use egg wash to brush the top of every biscuit.

Cover the air fryer 360's basket with parchment paper for the air fryer.

Fry for 4 minutes at 300 degrees Celsius.

For 2-5 minutes, change the temperature of an air fryer to 400 degrees before the biscuits develop a rich golden color.

Combine the honey and butter and blend well. If you like, include more or less.

Nutrients:

Amount per serving

Calories: 155kcal

Carbohydrates: 25g

Fat: 3g

Protein: 6g

2.26 Air Fried Puffed Egg Tarts:

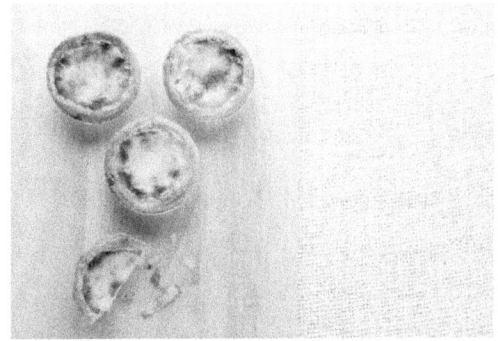

Cooking time: 20 minutes

Yield: 4 servings

Ingredients:

- All-purpose flour
- 3/4 cup shredded cheese
- 1 sheet frozen puff pastry, thawed
- 1 tbsp minced fresh chives or parsley, optional
- 4 large eggs

Instructions:

Unfold the pastry sheet on a floured table. Slice into 4 shapes of the square.

Put 2 squares in the basket of the air fryer and space them apart. Fry for about 10 mins or until the pastry is light brown.

Open the basket and press the centers of each square down to create an indentation using a spoon. Sprinkle each one with 3 tablespoons of cheese and gently break an egg into the middle of each one.

Air-fry for about 7 to 10 mins or until the ideal doneness of the eggs is attained. Set on waxed paper, move to a wire rack, and let cool for about 5 minutes. If needed, sprinkle with parsley. Serve it hot.

Nutrients:

Amount per serving

Calories 446

Carbohydrates 27.9g

Protein 14.2g

Fat 31g

2.27 Air Fried Breakfast Pockets:

Cooking time: 10 mins

Yield: 6-7 servings

Ingredients:

- 5 eggs
- One box puff pastry sheets
- 1/2 cup sausage crumbles, should be cooked
- 1/2 cup shredded cheddar cheese
- 1/2 cup cooked bacon

Instructions:

Eggs can be fried like normal scrambled eggs. If preferred, add meat to the mixture of eggs as you cook.

Take a cutting board, lay out pastry sheets, and cut out shapes of rectangles with a knife or a cookie cutter, make sure they all are smooth enough that they come together nicely.

On half of the pastry, Spoon favored the mixture of meat, egg, and cheese.

Place a rectangle of pastry on top of your mixture and then press the edges together with a fork to get a seal.

If you want a smooth, shiny pastry, spray it with spray oil, but it's basically optional.

Put pockets in an air-fryer 360's basket and cook at 370 degrees for about 8-10 minutes.

Monitor closely and check for desired doneness every 2-3 minutes.

Nutrients:

Serving: 1serving

Calories: 579kcal

Protein: 23g

Carbohydrates: 32g

Fat: 33g

2.28 Air Fried Hard Boiled Eggs:

Cooking time: 16 minutes

Yield: 6 eggs

Ingredients:

- 6 large-sized eggs

Instructions:

Put the eggs in the basket of an air fryer.

Air fry at 260 degrees for about 16 mins.

Extract the eggs by opening the power air fryer 360. Place them with cold water and ice in a container.

Enable 5 minutes for the eggs to let them cool. Peel them and serve.

Nutrients:

Serving: 1g

Calories: 72kcal

Fat: 5g

Protein: 6g

Chapter 03: Lunch

This chapter will help you to learn and experiment with the different basic varieties of recipes that are used on daily basis in the meals or lunch timings regarding air fried recipes of an air fryer. It definitely consists of an infinite number of options to try according to your taste buds. All the recipes are given in detail with the particular ingredients and nutrients.

3.1 Air Fried Southwest-Style Pork Loin:

Yield: 6 to 8 servings

Cooking time: 1: 15 mins

Ingredients:

- 2 jalapenos, seeded, stemmed, and coarsely chopped
- 1/2 cup chopped green onion tops
- 1/2 cup chopped onion
- 1/2 cup chopped cilantro
- 3 tablespoons canned chipotle peppers in the adobo sauce
- 1/2 cup vegetable oil
- 1 teaspoon salt
- 1 tablespoon plus 2 teaspoons Emeril's Southwest Essence
- One 2-pound boneless pork loin
- Cooked black beans, for serving (optional)
- Steamed rice, for serving (optional)

Instructions:

In the bowl of your food processor, mix the jalapenos, green onions, onions, cilantro, chipotle peppers, vegetable oil, and salt, and pulse to form a mostly smooth and soft mojo paste.

To seal the pork loin, cut a piece of aluminum foil big enough to put the pork on the foil. With the Southwest Essence, season the roast all over and then brush 3/4 of the mojo cup all over the roast. Wrap up and seal the foil around the roast and seal. Place the fryer in the basket and adjust the temperature to 350 F. Cook for 10 minutes, undisturbed. Reduce the heat to 300oF, uncover the roast, tuck the foil sides down such that the roast top is exposed, and then cook for 40 to 45 minutes, periodically testing to see that the roast does not get too brown on top (if so, put an extra piece of foil over the roast top so that it does not burn). When a thermometer of instant-read reads 145oF, the roast is ready.

Remove the basket from your air fryer and leave the roast to stand before slicing for at least 10 minutes.

Serve the roast in 1/2-inch pieces with the beans and rice as accompaniments, cut crosswise. When serving, any leftover mojo can be sprinkled over the roast.

Nutrients:

Amount per serving

Calories 45

Carbohydrates 0g

Protein 24g

Fats 8g

3.2 Meatball Pasta Bake:

Cooking time: 45 minutes

Yield: 6 servings

Ingredients:

- 2 tablespoons panko
- 1 pound ground beef
- 2 tablespoons whole milk
- 1/3 cup finely diced yellow onion
- 1 teaspoon chopped marjoram
- 3 cloves garlic, minced
- 1 teaspoon chopped basil
- 1/4 teaspoon crushed red pepper
- 3/4 teaspoon salt
- 1 large egg beaten
- 1 (23-ounce) jar of marinara sauce
- 1 tablespoon olive oil
- 4 ounces creme fraiche
- 1/2 cup freshly grated parmesan cheese
- 1 pound orecchiette or ditalini pasta, cooked al dente
- 1 1/4 cup grated mozzarella

Instructions:

Preheat the Emeril's Power Air Fryer 360 to 350 degree F.

Combine the milk and bread crumbs in a small bowl and allow them to stand for 5 minutes. Combine ground beef, garlic, crushed red pepper, onion, basil, salt, marjoram, and beaten egg in a separate, wide dish. Then add them to the bowl until the breadcrumbs are fluffy. Mix softly using your hands to combine.

Scoop 2 teaspoons of meat using a tiny scoop or spoon to make the meatballs and move them to a baking sheet.

Heat the olive oil in a wide saute pan over medium heat. When it is hot, add your meatballs in bunch and cook on all sides until golden brown, around 3 minutes per side. To a bowl, shift the meatballs and set them aside.

Heat your marinara sauce with creme fraiche in a medium-size sauce until warm, around for 5 minutes. For the meatballs, add the marinara and your pasta to the bowl and toss properly. Shift the meatballs and pasta to a baking dish and cover with the mozzarella and parmesan. Switch to the Emeril's Power Air Fryer 360 then bake for 15 or 20 minutes or until your cheese is nicely browned and the sauce starts to bubbles.

Nutrients:

Amount per serving

Calories 551.0

Total Carbohydrate 55.3 g

Dietary Fiber 5.8 g

Protein 34.1 g

3.3 Rosemary and Salt Roasted Shrimp with Garlic Butter Dipping Sauce:

Cooking time: 45 minutes

Yield: 4 servings

Ingredients:

- 3 to 4 pounds rock salt
- 8 sprigs fresh rosemary, break down in half, plus 1/4 teaspoon of minced leaves
- 20 large shrimp, shells on (about 2 pounds)
- 1/8 teaspoon red pepper flakes
- 1 stick unsalted butter
- 1 tablespoon lemon juice
- 1 tablespoon chopped garlic
- 1/4 teaspoon salt

Instructions:

At 400 degrees F set the Emeril Lagasse Air Fryer 360 of the setting to roast. To produce an even layer (1/4 of the salt), scatter plenty of the rock salt over the base of the baking sheet. Put it in the oven for 30 to 45 minutes to preheat.

Place the rosemary sprigs over the hot salt, spacing equally, and on top of each one place 1 shrimp. To cover entirely, top the shrimp with the leftover salt. Roast for around 10 to 12 minutes until the shrimps are pink and cooked through. With the remaining shrimp, repeat this process.

Make the dipping sauce while the shrimp are cooking. Melt your butter over medium heat in a shallow saucepan. Add the other ingredients and cook gently, around 5 minutes, until aromatic. Remove from the heat and bring in to serve warm in a beautiful bowl.

Remove the shrimp with the tongs to serve and put on a platter. (Likewise, before eating, peel the shrimp.) With the butter dip sauce on the side, eat the shrimp.

Nutrients:

Amount per serving

Calories 203.8

Fat 9.8g

Cholesterol 219.2mg

Carbohydrates 2.2g

Protein 25.6g

3.4 Snapper Fillets Baked in a Creole Sauce:

Cooking time: 45 minutes

Yield: 4 servings

Ingredients:

- Two 1 pound red snapper fillets
- 1 teaspoon cayenne pepper
- 1 tablespoon kosher salt
- 4 tablespoons) unsalted butter
- 3/4 cup chopped green bell peppers
- 2 1/2 cups chopped yellow onions
- 3/4 cup chopped celery
- 2 sprigs fresh thyme
- 3 bay leaves
- 1/2 cup chopped green onions (white and green parts)
- 2 tablespoons bleached all-purpose flour
- 1 tablespoon chopped garlic
- 2 cups chopped and seeded tomatoes
- 1 teaspoon Worcestershire sauce
- Chopped parsley, for garnish
- 2 cups chicken stock
- 1 teaspoon hot sauce

Instructions:

With the removal of any pin bones and scales, prepare the fish. With 1/2 teaspoon of cayenne pepper and 2 teaspoons of salt, season both fillets. When you are preparing the sauce, refrigerate the fish.

Melt butter over medium-high heat in a heavy medium stockpot. Add the onions, celery, cayenne, bell peppers, thyme, and bay leaves, and the remaining salt. Cook and stir regularly, for around 10 minutes, until the onions are golden and soft. Stir in the garlic and green onions and cook for around 1 minute, until fragrant. Stir in the flour and cook for around 2 minutes, stirring regularly, without browning the flour.

Add the Worcestershire, chicken stock, tomatoes, and pepper sauce. Cook for 10 minutes over medium heat. Remove your sauce from the heat and let it cool for 15 minutes, then add the parsley.

Preheat the 325 degrees F air fryer.

Butter the casserole dish. Onto the dish, pour the sauce, and afterward, nestle the fish fillets into your sauce. Bake for around 35 minutes, until the flesh is tender and cooked.

To sop up the sauce, serve it with warm bread.

Nutrients:

Amount per serving

Calories 295kcl

Carbs 8.3g

Protein 36.4g

Fat 12.6g

3.5 Buttermilk Fried Chicken:

Cooking time: 40 mins

Yield: Serves 6

Ingredients:

- 2 cups buttermilk
- 1 teaspoon sugar
- 2 tablespoons salt
- 1/2 teaspoon ground black pepper
- 6 chicken thighs
- 6 chicken legs
- 1 cup flour
- 6 cups crushed flaked corn cereal
- 6 eggs
- 1 tablespoon Emeril's Essence Seasoning

Instructions:

Into a large bowl, add the buttermilk. Add the buttermilk with sugar, salt, and black pepper. In the buttermilk, soak the chicken thighs and legs.

To a deep baking dish, add the flour.

Using a second dish to add the eggs and beat the eggs with a blade.

Add a third dish with the Emeril's Essence Seasoning and cereal crumbs.

Shake buttermilk off the bits of chicken and dredge the flour with the chicken, then the eggs, and eventually the crumbs. Put the pieces of chicken on the Crisper Tray.

Slide the Crisper Tray in the Shelf Position no. 2.

Keep rotating the Temperature Control Knob and the Time Control Knob to 191 degrees C for 40 minutes. To begin the cooking period, click the Start/Pause Button.

The chicken is ready to eat when the temperature of chicken reaches 71 degrees C internally. Click the Cancel key button and remove the Power Air Fryer 360 chicken.

Nutrients:

Amount per 4 oz

Calories 150

Carbohydrates 10g

Fats 10g

Protein 10g

3.6 Asian Oven Baked Flounder:

Cooking time: 50 minutes

Yield: 4 servings

Ingredients:

- 4 flounder fillets
- 2 tablespoons soy sauce
- 2 tablespoons sake
- 2 tablespoons fresh lime juice
- 2 teaspoons sesame oil
- 2 teaspoons minced fresh ginger
- 1 teaspoon honey
- 6 ounces shiitake mushrooms thinly sliced and stemmed
- 1 teaspoon lightly toasted sesame seeds
- 4 green onions, cut into 1-inch pieces, green tops only
- 1/2 large red pepper, cut into thin strips and seeded
- Sauteed Shiitake Mushrooms
- 1 large carrot, cut and peeled into 2-inch long matchstick strips
- Steamed rice, accompaniment

Instructions:

At 360 to 375 degrees F preheat your Emeril Lagasse Power Air Fryer. Cut 4 heavy aluminum foil squares wide enough to accommodate 1/4 of the vegetables and 1 flounder fillet. Lightly butter one side of each one and put it on a work surface.

In a baking dish, lay the fish flat. Whisk the sake, lime juice, soy sauce, ginger, honey, sesame oil, and sesame seeds together in a bowl. Pour over the fish and allow for up to 30 minutes to marinate. On each sheet of aluminum foil, place 1 fish fillet and cover with 1/4 of the peppers, mushrooms, carrots, onions, and marinade. Cover and arrange tightly on a baking sheet placed at shelf position no. 5. Bake for 15 to 20 minutes, until the fish is finally cooked and the vegetables are soft.

Remove and unwrap each packet from the oven. Shift to 4 wide plates the fish and vegetables and top with cooking juices. Serve with hot steamed rice and sauteed Shiitakes.

Nutrients:

Amount per serving

Calories 265.1kcl

Fat 13.6 g

Cholesterol 116.9 mg

Carbohydrates 3.7g

Protein 31.4g

3.7 Flank Steak:

Cooking time: 1hour

Yield: 4 Servings

Ingredients:

- 1 cup Extra Virgin Olive Oil
- 2 tablespoon Lime juice
- 0.6 cup sherry wine vinegar
- 1 cup chopped Cilantro
- 1 tablespoon chopped fresh marjoram leaves
- 0.25 cup chopped fresh basil leaves
- 3 tablespoon minced garlic
- 0.25 teaspoon crushed red pepper
- 2 tablespoon minced shallots
- 2.5 teaspoon Kosher Salt
- 1 3/4 to 2 lb flank steak
- 0.75 teaspoon fresh cracked black pepper
- Crusty bread

Instructions:

In the bowl of a food processor, combine the sherry vinegar, garlic, olive oil, lime juice, basil, cilantro, marjoram, and shallots. Pulse it until mixed well but not purée.

Add 1/2 tsp of smashed red pepper. 1/4 tsp. salt, and to complete your chimichurri sauce, apply black pepper and mix.

Switch from the processor to a non-reactive bowl with 1 cup of chimichurri sauce, cover with the plastic wrap and reserve for up to 6 hours at room temperature. Refrigerate the sauce before cooking the steak another day and return to room temperature before eating.

The steak is flavored with 1 tsp. Uh, salt and 1/4 tsp. black pepper on every side and put the steak in a big reseal able plastic bag. To the bag, apply the unreserved chimichurri sauce. For at least 2 hours, close the bag and put the steak in the refrigerator.

Remove it from the refrigerator when the steak is just ready to cook and let it rest for 30 mins. Wait until it arrives at room temperature. Brush the steak off with the excess chimichurri sauce and then put the steak on your pizza rack.

Slide into Shelf Position no. 2 the Pizza Rack. Choose the atmosphere for the Air Fry (205 ° C for 18 minutes). To begin the cooking period, click the Start Button. Cook until it exceeds the desired doneness.

Lay the steak on a neat cutting board and leave for 5-7 mins to rest the steak. Until being cut into small slices around the grain. Serve with crusty bread and 1 cup of chimichurri sauce on reserve.

Nutrients:

Amount per serving

Calories 219kcl

Protein 31.4 g

Carbohydrates 0 g

Fat 9.4 g

Fiber 0 g

3.8 Bacon and Corn Pudding:

Cooking time: 40-45 mins

Yield: 6 Servings

Ingredients:

- 4 strips of bacon
- 0.75 cup small diced onion
- Kernels from 2 ears of corn
- 0.5 cup small-diced red bell pepper
- 1 teaspoon Kosher Salt
- 0.25 cup small-diced celery
- 0.75 teaspoon Creole seasoning
- 2 teaspoon minced garlic
- 0.25 teaspoon ground cayenne pepper
- 1 teaspoon fresh thyme leaves
- 0.5 cup Heavy Cream
- 1.5 cup whole milk
- 3 large eggs
- 1 cup grated Monterey Jack
- 3 tablespoon finely grated Parmesan
- 3 cup cubed day-old bread
- 1 tablespoon butter

Instructions:

On the top of the stove, place a sauté pan of medium-size and fire the pan over medium heat and when the pan is hot, add the bacon and cook until most of the fat has been produced (3-4 mins) while stirring as needed.

In the pan, add the onion, Creole seasoning, corn, bell pepper, salt, celery, and ground cayenne pepper and cook until tender (about 5 mins.). Garlic and thyme are then applied and the pan is removed from the heat.

In a medium-size bowl, add the cream, milk, and eggs and whisk to combine. Fold in a mixture of bread, Monterey Jack, and onion. Set it aside for 5 minutes to allow some of the liquid to be consumed by the bread.

Grease the 9 x 9 3-qt. Apply the butter to the casserole dish and add the pudding mixture to your pan.

Slide your Pizza Rack into Shelf Position no. 6. Place the casserole dish on the pizza rack. Select the setting for baking (325 °F/165 °C). Adjust the cooking time to about 20 minutes. To begin the cooking period, click the Start Button.

Sprinkle the Parmesan over the pudding evenly until the cooking period is over.

Set the Bake Setting. Set the temperature for cooking to 149° C then set the cooking time to about 10 minutes. To begin the cooking period, click the Start Button.

Remove the pudding from Power Air Fryer 360 when the time of cooking is over and allow it to cool for at least 30 minutes till you serve.

Nutrients:

Amount per 214g

Calories 217kcl

Fat 19g

Cholesterol 169mg

Carbohydrates 25g

Protein 8.5g

3.9 New York-Style Thin Crust Pizza:

Cooking time: 40-45mins

Yield: 2 Servings

Ingredients:

- 1 tablespoon olive oil
- 28 ounce canned whole peeled tomatoes, pureed &drained
- 1 onion, chopped
- 1 sprig fresh thyme
- 0.5 teaspoon freshly ground black pepper
- 0.5 teaspoon salt
- 0.25 cup extra virgin olive oil plus
- 1 pound pizza dough, divided into two balls
- 1 tablespoon extra-virgin olive oil, which is divided
- Cornmeal, for dusting
- 1 cup freshly grated Parmigiano-Reggiano
- 0.5 cup fresh basil leaves
- 1 pound mozzarella, thickly sliced 1/4-in.

Instructions:

Put a small saucepan on top of the burner. Heat 1 tablespoon over medium heat your olive oil. Then add the garlic and onion and cook until tender (about 3 mins).

Add the tomatoes, salt, thyme sprig, and black pepper, and cook for 20 minutes. Then from the heat, remove the saucepan.

Stir in around 1 tablespoon the extra virgin olive oil and reserve the sauce before ready for use.

Place the dough on a cornmeal-dusted surface. Roll the dough to match on the crisper tray (1/8-1/4 in. thick) using a finely floured rolling pin.

Use 2 tablespoons of olive oil to brush the dough. Over the dough, spoon the sauce evenly, leaving a 1/2-inches border. Place the basil leaves on top of the sauce and the mozzarella and the Parmigiano-Reggiano.

Place the Crisper Tray on the Pizza. Slide the Crisper Tray into the Shelf Position no. 5. Set the setting for the pizza (190 ° C for 20 minutes). To begin the cooking period, click the Start Button.

Slide the Crisper Tray into the Shelf Position no. 1 when the cooking period is complete. Set the setting for the pizza. Set the temperature for cooking to 205° C and set the time of cooking to 2 minutes. To begin the cooking period, click the Start Button.

Break the pizza into six slices after the cooking period is done, and eat instantly.

Nutrients:

Amount per serving

Calories 208kcal

Fat 9.27g

CARBOHYDRATES 21.79g

Protein 9.25g

3.10 Reuben Sandwich:

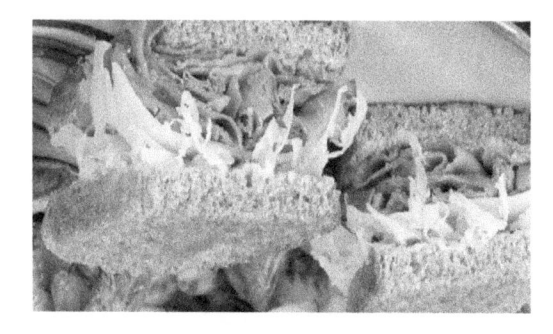

Cooking time: About 6 hours

Yield: 4 Servings

Ingredients:

- 3-pound corned beef brisket
- 1 cup mayonnaise
- 12-ounce beer
- 0.25 cup chili sauce
- 1 tablespoon minced celery
- 1 tablespoon minced yellow onion
- 1 tablespoon minced parsley
- 0.5 teaspoon dry mustard
- 1 tablespoon Heavy Cream
- 0.5 teaspoon hot pepper sauce
- 1 pound Sauerkraut
- 8 slice rye sourdough bread
- 0.75 cup butter, softened
- 16 slice Swiss Cheese

Instructions:

Put the corned beef in a 4.5-qt. Dutch oven which fits in the Power Air Fryer 360 inside and tops the beer with the corned beef with enough water to cover your corned beef.

Slide your Pizza Rack into the Shelf Position no. 6. Place the Dutch oven on your pizza rack.

Set the Slow Cook (225° F/107° C) setting. Set the time to cook for 6 hrs. To begin the cooking period, click the Start Button.

Combine the mayonnaise, yellow sauce, chili sauce, onion, parsley, celery, mustard, heavy cream, and hot pepper sauce. Refrigerate the dressing before you finish cooking the corned beef.

Remove the corned beef then slice it thinly before the cooking time runs out.

With 2 slices of Swiss cheese per bread slice, butter the bread slices. Cover the cheese with the sauerkraut, corned beef, and 2 tbsp. of Russian dressing. Then the leftover Swiss cheese and the remainder of the bread slices are added (buttered side up).

Slide the Pizza Rack into Shelf Position no.6.

Choose the Toast Setting (about 4mins. 40secs.). To begin the cooking period, click the Start Button. Cook until it is crispy and golden.

Nutrients:

Amount per serving

Carbohydrates 52 g

Fat 38 g

Protein 58 g

Fiber 4 g

3.11 Roasted Garlic White Pizza with Garlic Sauce:

Cooking time: 40-45mins

Yield: 8 Servings

Ingredients:

- 2 tablespoon unsalted butter
- 1 cup whole milk
- 2 tablespoon all-purpose flour
- 0.25 teaspoon ground cayenne pepper
- 0.25 teaspoon salt
- 3 heads roasted garlic
- 1 cup warm water (105° F–115° F)
- 2 tablespoon Extra Virgin Olive Oil
- 1 teaspoon Honey
- 1.25-ounce active dry yeast
- 8-ounce fresh mozzarella cheese, sliced
- 2.5 cup unbleached all-purpose flour
- 4 ounce grated Fontina cheese
- 30 pieces sun-dried tomatoes
- 0.5 cup finely grated Parmigiano-Reggiano cheese
- 2 tablespoon chopped fresh basil leaves

Instructions:

Put a pot of sauce on top of the burner. Melt the butter over medium-high heat in the saucepot and then cook your flour for 2-3 mins.

Whisk the milk in 2 teaspoons of all-purpose flour.

Garnish with garlic, ground cayenne pepper, and 1/4 tsp salt and cook for 15 mins under low heat. The béchamel is made.

In a bowl, mix the honey, water, and olive oil together. Add yeast, all-purpose unbleached flour, and 1 tsp salt; mix; knead until smooth. For 20 mins, put the bowl aside.

Divide the dough of pizza in half and fit on the pizza rack to fit each half. On the pizza rack, put one of the halves. Put the Fontina, mozzarella, and Parmigiano-Reggiano cheeses and sun-dried tomatoes on top of the dough.

Slide the Pizza Rack into the Shelf Position no. 5. Select a setting for pizza (20-min. cooking time). Set the temperature of cooking to 165 °C. To begin the cooking period, click the Start Button.

Repeat the cooking phase on the second pizza as the cooking time runs out.

Cover with the parsley, basil, and crushed red pepper when both the pizzas are finished cooking.

Nutrients:

Amount per serving

Calories 451.5kcl

Protein 22.4 g

Carbohydrates 23.8g

Fats 27g

3.12 Roasted Salmon:

Cooking time: 20mins

Yield: 4 Servings

Ingredients:

- 2-pound salmon fillet
- 2 tablespoon Emeril's Essence Seasoning
- 1 tablespoon fresh lemon juice

Instructions:

Place the baking sheet with the salmon. With Emeril's Essence Seasoning and lemon juice, season the salmon.

Slide your pizza rack into Shelf Position no.1. Place the pizza rack on top of the baking pan.

Rotate the Program Selection Knob to roast setting (175° C). Rotate the Time Control Knob to twenty minutes. To begin the cooking period, click the Start/Pause Button.

Nutrients:

Amount per serving

Calories 337.9kcl

Protein 31.6 g

Carbohydrates 15.7 g

Total Fat 16.5 g

Cholesterol 80.5 mg

3.13 Blue Cheese-Stuffed Burgers:

Cooking time: 25-30mins

Yield: 4 Servings

Ingredients:

- 2-pound of ground beef
- 1 teaspoon salt
- 2 tbsp. of Worcestershire
- 4 brioche buns
- 0.5 tsp. black pepper which is grounded
- 8 tbsp. of blue cheese that is crumbled
- 4 slice red onions
- 4 slice bacon, chopped &cooked
- 4 Bibb of lettuce leaves
- 0.25 cup of butter, that is softened
- 8 slices of Tomatoes

Instructions:

In a bowl, blend together the Worcestershire sauce, ground beef, black pepper, and salt.

Divide four balls of your beef mixture and divide every ball into half.

On the counter, press your meat. Stuff the bacon with ½ of the beef and 2 tablespoon of blue cheese for each burger and unstuffed beef on top. Cover the sides of the burgers.

Slide into the Shelf Position no. 2 the Pizza Rack. Place your burgers on your pizza rack.

Rotate the Air Fry setting of the Program Knob of Selection (205 ° C for about 18mins.). To begin the cooking period, click the Start/Pause Button.

When you have finished cooking the burger, remove it from your pizza rack and put them aside.

Slide into the Shelf Position no. 1 the pizza rack. Butter and put brioche buns on your pizza rack.

Rotate Program knob of selection (205 ° C for about 10 minutes) to the broil setting. To begin your cooking period, click the Start/Pause Button. Broil your buns until they're golden. Then assemble your burgers with some red onions, tomatoes, meat, and lettuce after removing the buns.

Nutrients:

Amount per serving

Calories 589.5kcl

Carbohydrates 32.7 g

Protein 34.1 g

Total Fat 34.6 g

Cholesterol 121.3 mg

3.14 Air Fried Citrus and Honey Glazed Ham:

Cooking time: 45 minutes

Yield: 6 to 8 servings

Ingredients:

- One 2 1/2-pound fully cooked boneless smoked ham
- 1/4 cup honey
- 1/2 cup light brown sugar
- 2 tablespoons orange juice
- 2 tablespoons Dijon mustard
- 2 tablespoons cider vinegar
- 1/4 teaspoon ground cinnamon
- 1/4 teaspoon ground ginger
- 1/4 teaspoon ground nutmeg
- 1/4 teaspoon ground cloves
- 1/4 teaspoon cayenne
- 1/4 teaspoon smoked paprika
- 1/4 teaspoon salt

Instructions:

Let the ham out of its packaging and wipe it dry. Break the aluminum foil into two parts wide enough to wrap the ham and put the ham on top of the foil.

In a shallow tub, mix the remaining ingredients and whisk them to incorporate. Drizzle over the ham with 1/4 cup of the glaze, then cover the ham in the foil and put it in the air-fryer basket. Fix the temperature and cook for 15 minutes at 320°F.

Remove your basket from the air fryer and gently open the foil package to reveal the top and edges of the ham, forcing the foil edges away, however, make sure the ham is still laying on the foil. Draw more glazes on the ham, and cook at 320 °F for 5 minutes. With more glazes remove the ham and clean again. Repeat this 2 more times, 15 to 20 minutes in all, before the ham is nicely glazed on the edges. Take note that the ham should not overcook or it may dry out.

Take the ham from the air fryer and let it sit for a little time, then serve.

Nutrients:

Amount per serving

Carbohydrates: 12g

Protein: 54g

Calories: 519kcal

Fat: 27g

3.15 Air Fried New York Strip Steak with Red Wine Sauce:

Cooking time: 15 to 20 minutes

Yield: 2 to 4 servings

Ingredients:

- One 1 pound NY strip steak that is about 1-inch thick
- 1 tablespoon unsalted butter
- Salt and pepper
- 3 tablespoons heavy cream
- ¼ cup chopped shallots
- ½ cup dry red wine
- 1 tablespoon minced garlic
- 2 teaspoons beef bouillon base

Instructions:

Season your steak with pepper and salt and move to the Emeril Air Fryer basket and set for 10-12 minutes at 400 degrees F for a medium-rare time, or until the optimal temperature is achieved. Switch the steak halfway through the cooking time, so that it cooks equally. When cooked, give 10 minutes for the steak to relax.

When the steak is resting, prepare the sauce: In a saucepan, melt the butter over medium heat. Season with pepper and salt; add garlic and shallots and sauté for one minute. Stir in the red wine and get it to a boil. Reduce the fire to a mild and add the beef bouillon. For 2 minutes more, or before the bouillon is dissolved, simmer. Heavy cream is applied and baked for one min longer. Remove from the heat and keep it warm.

Break the steak into slices and eat with Red Wine Sauce.

Nutrients:

Amount per serving

Calories: 649kcl

Protein: 69.3g

Carbohydrates: 7.5g

Fat: 33.9g

3.16 Air Fried Roasted Duck:

Cooking time: 15mins

Yield: 2 servings

Ingredients:

- Orange sauce
- 1 fully cooked half-duck

Instructions:

Put your half-duck in the basket of your air fryer.

Cook for 12 to 15 minutes at 183°C.

Drizzle and eat with orange sauce.

Nutrients:

Amount per serving

Calories: 2313kcal

Protein: 66g

Carbohydrates: 13g

Fat: 220g

3.17 Grilled Chicken Breast Strips:

Cooking time: 30mins

Yield: 5-6 servings

Ingredients:

- Extra Virgin Olive Oil
- 2 Boneless and Skinless Chicken Breasts
- Applewood Smoked Salt
- Mrs. Dash Chicken Grilling Blend
- Freshly Ground Black Pepper

Instructions:

To bake, turn the selection dial.

Place your Pizza Rack in the Power Air Fryer 360 position for Pizza, the second up from the lowest rack location.

Turn the dial to a temperature of 425° F.

Move to 28 minutes on the Time Dial.

The start button is pushed.

The pre-heating of the Power Air Fryer 360 will start.

When starting pre-heated:

Cover the oil with the chicken. Cover chicken with some spices. Position the Chicken on the Crisper Tray and then wait for the completion of pre-heating.

Click the Start/Pause button until pre-heating is done. Then turn your time dial back to the complete 28 minutes you picked initially.

To collect the drippings, put the baking sheet on the pizza rack.

Position the Crisper Tray in your Power Air Fryer 360 on the Air Fry rack level. This is just above your Pizza Rack top, the level of the rack.

Close and click the Start/Pause Button on the Control Air Fryer 360. This will cook to initiate the cooking.

Give it some time to cook properly.

Confirm that the temperature of the meat is at least 165° F.

Nutrients:

Amount per serving

Calories: 100kcal

Carbohydrates: 1.00g

Fat: 2.00g

Protein: 18.00g

3.18 Air Fried St. Louis Spareribs:

Cooking time: 1hour 20mins

Yield: 2 serving

Ingredients:

- Pork Rub of choice
- 1 Slab of St. Louis Spareribs
- Hickory Smoked Sea Salt
- Apple Juice for spritzing
- Cooking Spray
- Fresh Ground Black Pepper

Instructions:

Turn to roast the selection dial.

Place your Pizza Rack in the Emeril's Power Air Fryer position for Pizza, the second up from lowest rack position.

Switch to a temperature of 375 °F.

Switch to 1 hour, 20 minutes on the Time Dial.

Then push the start button.

The pre-heating of the Power Air Fryer 360 will start.

During pre-heated:

Use Cooking Spray to spray the baking pan. Break the slab into quarters with the ribs. Cover it with spices. Place the ribs outside the oven on the baking pan and wait to finish the pre-heating.

Click the Start/Pause button until pre-heating is done. Then go back to a complete 1 hour, 20 minutes on the Time Dial.

Place your pizza rack in the baking pan.

Close and click the Start/Pause Button on the Control Air Fryer 360.

Click the Start/Pause button after 45 minutes to interrupt the cooking. Then spritz the apple juice on the ribs.

To begin cooking, click the Start or Pause button.

Enable it to complete the rest of the cooking period.

The meat temperature should be tested at a minimum of 165 ° F., but it should be a little over 190 ° F.

Nutrients:

Amount per serving

Calories: 375kcal

Protein: 18g

Carbohydrates: 12g

Fats: 27g

3.19 Southern Fried Chicken:

Cooking time: 20mins

Yield: 5-6 servings

Ingredients:

- 8-10 Chicken Drumettes
- 2 cups white all-purpose flour
- 1 cup buttermilk
- 1 Tbs black pepper
- 1 Tbs garlic powder
- 1 tsp salt
- 1 tsp creole seasoning
- 1 Tbs paprika
- 1 tsp onion powder
- 1 tsp cumin

Instructions:

Soak the chicken in buttermilk in the fridge for about 2 hours.

Combine the flour & seasonings in a separate bowl and blend properly.

Remove the buttermilk chicken and put it on a tray.

Dip each chicken piece into flour mixture, preceded by the buttermilk, and then into the flour mixture once more.

Put every piece of chicken in the chicken basket.

Place the basket in the Power Air Fryer.

Click and scroll over the M button to the chicken icon.

At 360 degrees, change the cooking time to 20 minutes and begin.

To avoid any sticking, turn the chicken with tongs around every 5 minutes and serve immediately.

Nutrients:

Amount per serving

Calories: 164kcal

Protein: 20g

Carbohydrates: 12g

Fats: 9g

3.20 Air Fried Roasted Broccoli:

Cooking time: 15 minutes

Yield: 4 servings

Ingredients:

- 1 teaspoon Herbes de Provence seasoning optional
- 3-4 cups fresh broccoli florets
- Salt and pepper to taste
- 1 tablespoon olive oil or cooking oil spray

Instructions:

Drizzle with olive oil the broccoli or spray with the cooking oil. The seasonings are sprinkled throughout.

Spray a basket of the air fryer with cooking oil. Load up your broccoli. Cook at 360 degrees for 5-8 minutes.

Open your air fryer and check the broccoli until it has cooked for five minutes. To make sure the broccoli is not overcooked, use your judgment.

Nutrients:

Amount per serving

Calories: 61kcal

Protein: 3g

Carbohydrates: 4g

Fat: 3g

3.21 Air Fried Panko Breaded Chicken Drumsticks:

Cooking time: 22 minutes and Buttermilk refrigeration for 30 minutes

Yield: 4 servings

Ingredients:

- 3 pounds chicken drumsticks
- 1 cup panko breadcrumbs
- 1/4 cup buttermilk
- 2 teaspoons McCormick's Grill Mates Montreal Chicken Seasoning
- Cooking oil spray
- Salt and pepper to taste

Instructions:

Drizzle with the buttermilk the chicken. The chicken may be put in a bowl. For 30 minutes, refrigerate.

Spray a basket of air fryer with cooking oil.

With chicken seasoning, pepper, and salt to taste, apply the panko breadcrumbs to a dish and stir

Dredge your buttermilk chicken in the mixture of the panko breadcrumbs. With cooking oil, brush all sides of the chicken.

Put the chicken in the basket of an air fryer and cook at 380 degrees for 10 minutes.

Place the air fryer open and turn the chicken over. Cook the chicken until the chicken hits an internal temperature of about 165 degrees for a further 10-14 minutes.

Before serving, let it cool.

Nutrients:

Amount per serving

Protein: 56g

Carbohydrates: 20g

Calories: 466kcal

Fat: 18g

3.22 Turkey and Hot Sausage Chili:

Cooking time: 2 hours

Yield: 8 servings

Ingredients:

- 1 pound ground turkey
- 1 tablespoon vegetable oil
- 12 ounces hot Italian sausage, crumbled and removed from casings
- 1 ½ cups chopped yellow onions
- 2 teaspoons Emeril's Original Essence
- ½ cup chopped green bell peppers
- 2 tablespoons minced garlic
- ½ cup chopped, Anaheim chilies or peeled and roasted green Poblano
- 2 tablespoons chili powder
- ½ teaspoon salt
- 1 ½ teaspoon ground cumin
- One 12-ounce lager beer
- 2 cups cooked pinto beans, rinsed and drained or canned beans,
- One 28-ounce can of chopped tomatoes and juice
- ¼ cup chopped fresh cilantro
- Tortilla chips
- 2 cups grated Monterey Jack cheese

Instructions:

Preheat the oil in a big pot in the air fryer. Add the sausage, turkey, and essence, and cook for 6 to 8 minutes until the meat is not pink anymore. Add the bell peppers, onions, and chilies, and cook for around 3 minutes, in the air fryer until tender. Apply the garlic, chili powder, salt and cumin then cook for 1 minute. Open the air fryer and add the tomatoes and beer. Lower the temperature of the air fryer and cook for 45 minutes to one hour.

Remove it from the air fryer and add cilantro. To keep it warm before ready to eat, adjust seasoning to how much you like and cover.

Ladle them into wide bowls to eat and top each serving with 1/4 cup of cheese. Serve it with tortilla chips.

Nutrients:

Amount per serving

Calories: 208kcal

Carbohydrates: 31g

Fats: 4g

Proteins: 12.2g

3.23 Juicy Air Fried Cheeseburgers:

Cooking time: 20 minutes

Yield: 4 servings

Ingredients:

- 1 teaspoon liquid smoke
- 1 pound 80/20 ground chuck beef
- 4 buns
- 1 teaspoon Worcestershire sauce
- Salt and pepper
- 1 1/2 tablespoons Weber Burger Seasoning
- 4 slices of cheese

Instructions:

The liquid smoke, burger sauce, Worcestershire, pepper, and salt are seasoned with the ground beef to taste. Shape 4 patties for burgers

Use the air fryer to cook the burgers.

Cook the burgers at 360 degrees for 8 minutes.

Place the air fryer open and turn the burgers over. For an extra 3-4 minutes, cook.

To decide whether they are completed frying, check the interior of the burgers. To analyze the color, you may put a fork or knife in the middle.

Top a slice of cheese for each burger. Cook it for two more minutes, or until cheese is melted.

Serve on the buns.

Nutrients:

Amount per serving

Calories: 524

Carbohydrates: 22g

Total Fat: 32g

Protein: 30g

3.24 Air Fried Bacon Grilled Cheese:

Cooking time: 12 minutes

Yield: 2 servings

Ingredients:

- 1 tablespoon butter melted
- 4 slices of bread
- 2 slices mild cheddar cheese
- 2 slices mozzarella cheese
- 5-6 slices of cooked bacon

Instructions:

In the microwave, heat the butter for 10 to15 sec to soften.

Then spread the butter over one side of each bread slice.

Insert a piece of buttered bread (the butter side down) into the basket of the air fryer.

Place the rest of the ingredients in the order below: cheddar cheese slice then cooked bacon slice then mozzarella cheese slice and then top with another bread slice.

Cook it at 370 degrees for 4 minutes.

Open a fryer in the air. Flip your sandwich. For an extra 3 minutes, cook.

Remove and then serve.

Nutrients:

Serving: 1sandwich

Protein: 25g

Calories: 486kcal

Carbohydrates: 25g

Fat: 26g

3.25 Air Fried Honey Glazed Ham:

Cooking time: 50 minutes

Yield: 12 servings

Ingredients:

- 1/3 cup honey
- 3-4 pound boneless fully cooked ham
- 1/4 teaspoon ground cloves
- 1/4 cup brown sweetener

Instructions:

In a saucepan, mix the brown sweetener, honey, and ground cloves over medium-high flame. Remove from the heat and whisk before the sweetener has been absorbed.

You should keep it on during the primary cooking procedure if the ham comes with the netting. With around 1/4 of your honey glaze mixture, glaze the ham by using a cooking brush and seal the ham securely in foil.

Then place the ham wrapped in foil in the basket of an air fryer. Fry for 40 minutes at 300 degrees.

Open the air fryer and cut from around the ham the foil and the netting. Again, glaze the ham. To drizzle over individual ham slices, you should reserve almost 1/4 of your glaze mixture here.

Fry the ham for an extra 5 minutes at 400 degrees.

The ham can be removed from the air fryer. Until slicing, allow the ham to rest for 10 minutes.

Nutrients:

Amount per serving

Calories: 213kcal

Protein: 20g

Carbohydrates: 11g

Fat: 9g

3.26 Air Fried Juicy Cornish Hens:

Cooking time: 45 minutes

Yield: 4 servings

Ingredients:

- 2 Cornish hens
- 1 teaspoon smoked paprika
- 1 teaspoon garlic powder
- 1/2 teaspoon ground thyme
- 1 teaspoon poultry seasoning
- 1/2 teaspoon ground rosemary
- Salt and pepper to taste
- 2-4 slices fresh lemon
- Cooking oil

Instructions:

Spray a basket of air fryers with cooking oil. Put in the basket the lemon slices.

Dry Pat the Cornish Hens. Use towels made of paper.

With oil, rub all sides of each bird. Sprinkle all sides with the spices and seasoning.

On top of the lemons, put the breast side of Cornish hens down into the air fryer. You don't want to overcook those legs.

Fry for 25 minutes at 350 degrees.

Open the basket and then flip the hens out of the grain. Cook for a further 10-15 minutes or until a temperature of about 165 degrees has hit your Cornish hens internally. Use a thermometer for meat. Adjust and add extra cooking time if needed, if you like very crispy skin.

Place the thermometer of the meat in the chicken's thickest portion, which is usually the region of the chicken thigh. You should even test the breast and make sure that the whole chicken is completely cooked.

Remove your hens from the basket of the air fryer and put them on a plate to rest it for at least 15 minutes until the chicken is sliced. This will cause the moisture to evenly redistribute within the chicken.

Nutrients:

Serving: 0.5hen

Protein: 48g

Calories: 530kcal

Fat: 39g

3.27 Air Fried Beef Meatballs BBQ:

Cooking time: 25 minutes

Yield: 5 servings

Ingredients:

- ½ cup chopped onions
- ½ cup of almond meal
- 2 cloves of garlic
- 1 pound of ground chuck beef
- ¼ cup of shredded cheese (cheddar)
- 1/2 cup sugar-free BBQ Sauce
- 1 egg
- 1 teaspoon Worcestershire sauce
- Pepper and salt
- 1 teaspoon McCormick's Grill Mates Steak Seasoning

Instructions:

In a large bowl, add the beef chuck, egg, onions, almond meal, garlic, Worcestershire sauce, cheddar, and seasonings.

Combine all ingredients using washed hands and shape one wide ball.

Then use a spoon to bring 10 meatballs that are smaller together. To avoid contamination, you should set them on the parchment paper.

Use your air fryer and load the meatballs. Spray a basket of air fryers with the cooking oil.

Cook your meatballs at 365 degrees for about 8 minutes.

Keep your air fryer open and turn the meatballs over.

Cook until your meatballs hit a temperature of about 165 degrees internally for an extra 5-8 minutes.

Remove from your air fryer the meatballs and drizzle with BBQ sauce.

Nutrients:

Serving: 2meatballs

Calories: 336kcal

Carbohydrates: 3g

Protein: 21g

Fat: 26g

3.28 Air Fried Garlic Roasted Green Beans:

Cooking time: 10 minutes

Yield: 4 servings

Ingredients:

- 3/4-1 pound fresh green beans
- 1 teaspoon garlic powder
- 1 tablespoon olive oil
- Salt and pepper to taste

Instructions:

Drizzle over your green beans the olive oil. The seasonings are sprinkled throughout. Toss it to coat it.

Put your green beans in the basket of an air fryer.

Cook your green beans at 370 degrees for 7-8 minutes. Toss halfway through the estimated cooking period for the basket.

Remove your green beans and eat.

Nutrients:

Serving: 1g

Calories: 45kcal

Carbohydrates: 3g

Protein: 1g

Fat: 3g

3.29 Air Fried Homemade Crispy French Fries:

Cooking time: 30 minutes

Yield: 4 servings

Ingredients:

- 2 1/2 pound each, potatoes cut lengthwise and peeled
- Salt and pepper
- Seasoning salt
- 1 tbsp olive oil

Instructions:

Layer the sliced potatoes with cold water in a wide bowl.

Allow the potatoes for 30mins, to soak in the water.

Drain from the bowl the water. Dry the fries with paper towels fully.

Use olive oil to cover the fries. In a wide bowl, you should throw them or spray the fries on a flat surface and then coat them. Sprinkle with salt, pepper, and optional salt for seasoning.

To the Air Fryer basket, add half of the fries. To 380 degrees, set the temperature and cook for 15 to 20 minutes. Set a 10-minute timer and pause at the 10-minute mark and shake the basket (once).

If you need the fries to be crisper, give them some time to prepare. Remove them if the fries appear crisp before 15 minutes. Cook the remaining portion as the first half finished.

Before serving it let it cool.

Nutrients:

Amount per serving

Calories: 162kcal

Protein: 4g

Carbohydrates: 32g

Fat: 2g

3.30 Air Fried Crispy Fish Sandwich:

Cooking time: 20 minutes

Yield: 2 servings

Ingredients:

- 2 tablespoons all-purpose flour
- 1/4 teaspoon pepper
- 1/2 teaspoon garlic powder
- 1/4 teaspoon salt
- 1 tablespoon fresh lemon juice
- 1 egg
- 1/2 tablespoon mayo
- 1/2 cup panko bread crumbs
- 10 oz cod fillets Sliced in half to make 2 fillets
- Cooking oil
- Primal Kitchen Tartar Sauce
- 2 buns

Instructions:

For the Breading:

Set up a station for cooking. In a bowl wide enough to dredge the fish, apply the flour, salt, garlic powder, and pepper.

In a separate bowl wide enough to dredge the fish, apply the mayo, egg, and lemon juice to it. The egg is beaten and the components are mixed.

Add to a different bowl the panko breadcrumbs.

In the flour, dredge the fish, then the egg mixture and the breadcrumbs.

For air frying:

Spray the basket of the air fryer with cooking oil and bring the fish to your basket.

Spritz the surface of cooking oil on the fish.

Cook at 400 degrees for 8-10 minutes, until crisp and golden. Do so at 5 minutes if you want to flip your fish and then begin to air fry until it is crisp and golden.

Nutrients:

Serving: 1sandwich

Calories: 494kcal

Protein: 28g

Carbohydrates: 48g

Fat: 21g

3.31 Air Fried Buffalo Cauliflower:

Cooking time: 20 minutes

Yield: 4 servings

Ingredients:

- 1 head cauliflower cut in small bites
- Salt and pepper to taste
- 1/2 cup buffalo sauce
- Cooking oil
- 1 tablespoon butter melted

Instructions:

Spray a basket of air fryer with cooking oil.

In a bowl, combine the buffalo sauce, melted butter, and season with salt and pepper. Stir to mix.

Use the air fryer and add your cauliflower bites. Use cooking oil to spray. Cook at 400 degrees for 7 minutes.

Open an air fryer and put a large mixing bowl with the cauliflower. Drizzle all over the buffalo mixture and butter and stir.

Add the cauliflower to an air fryer. Cook at 400 degrees for an extra 7-8 minutes, before the cauliflower wings become crisp.

Remove from the air fryer the cauliflower and serve.

Nutrients:

Amount per serving

Calories: 101kcal

Protein: 3g

Carbohydrates: 4g

Fat: 7g

3.32 Air Fryer Pepperoni Pizza:

Cooking time: 10minutes

Yield: 1 pizza

Ingredients:

- 1 whole-wheat pita
- 1/8th cup mozzarella cheese
- 2 tbsp pizza sauce or marinara
- 1/8th cup cheddar cheese
- Olive oil spray
- 8 slices pepperoni
- 1 tbsp chopped parsley

Instructions:

On top of pita bread drizzle, the sauce then loads the shredded cheese and pepperoni on top.

Use an olive oil spray to spray the surface of the pizza.

Place it at 400 degrees in the Air Fryer for about 8 minutes. At the 6-7 minute point, check-in on the pizza, and make sure it is not overcooked.

Remove from the Air Fryer the pizza.

Nutrients:

Serving: 1pizza

Protein: 17g

Carbohydrates: 33g

Calories: 334kcal

Fat: 14g

3.33 Fried Shrimp Po' Boy Sandwich:

Cooking time: 30 minutes

Servings: 4

Ingredients:

- 1 pound shrimp that deveined
- 1/4 cup buttermilk
- 1 teaspoon Creole Seasoning
- 1/2 cup Louisiana Fish Fry Coating
- 4 French bread hoagie rolls
- 8 tomato slices
- Cooking oil spray
- 2 cups shredded iceberg lettuce

For Remoulade Sauce:

- 1 tsp minced garlic
- 1/2 cup mayo
- 1/2 lemon juice
- 1/2 tsp Creole Seasoning
- 1 tsp Worcestershire
- 1 tsp Dijon mustard
- 1 green onion chopped
- 1 tsp hot sauce

Instructions:

Combine all of the Remoulade Sauce components in a shallow bowl. Before cooking the shrimp, refrigerate it.

For 30 minutes, marinate the shrimp in buttermilk and Creole seasoning.

Add the fried fish to the bowl. Remove the shrimp from bags and put each of them in the fish fry. Add the shrimp to the basket of an air fryer.

Spray a basket of air fryers with cooking oil then add the shrimp to the basket of an air fryer.

Spritz with the cooking oil the shrimp.

Cook the shrimp at 400 degrees for 5 minutes. Open the basket and then flip to the other face of the shrimp. Cook it for 3-5 more minutes or until it is crisp.

On the French bread, scatter the remoulade sauce. Add the tomato and lettuce slices and then the shrimp.

Nutrients:

Amount per serving

Calories: 437kcal

Protein: 24g

Carbohydrates: 55g

Fat: 12g

3.34 Air Fried Parmesan Breaded Chicken Tenders:

Cooking time: 25 minutes

Servings: 4

Ingredients:

- 1/3 cup grated parmesan cheese
- 1 pound skinless chicken breast sliced into strips
- 1/3 cup breadcrumbs
- 1/4 cup all-purpose flour
- 1 egg
- 1 teaspoon Italian Seasoning
- Cooking oil spray
- Salt and pepper to taste

Instructions:

In different bowls placed the eggs, breadcrumbs, and flour.

In a bowl of breadcrumbs, apply the grated parmesan, salt, Italian seasoning, and pepper to taste then stir.

Cover the chicken breasts with sliced flour, then the egg, then the breadcrumbs.

Then spray the chicken tenders with some cooking oil.

Use the air fryer basket and add the chicken tenders. Cook at 400 degrees for 8 minutes.

Flip the tenders after opening the basket. Cook for a further 6-8 minutes or until the tenders of the chicken are crisp.

Nutrients:

Serving: 1serving

Calories: 239kcal

Protein: 29g

Carbohydrates: 13g

Fat: 9g

3.35 Air Fried Mac and Cheese Balls:

Cooking time: 8-10mins

Yield: 8-10 balls

Ingredients:

- 6 cup Macaroni Noodles, cooled and cooked
- 1 Can Ricos Gourmet Nacho Cheese
- 1 cup Shredded Cheese
- 3 Eggs, beaten
- 1 Can Ricos Queso Blanco Cheese
- 1 cup Milk
- 1 cup Flour
- 1 cup Panko Breadcrumbs

Instructions:

Combine the cheese, macaroni noodles, and Ricos Cheese in a broad mixing bowl and combine well.

Scoop the macaroni on a cookie sheet and put it in the refrigerator for about 30 minutes or in the freezer for 10 minutes, using a big spoon or ice cream scoop.

Take them out of the freezer or refrigerator and roll them into balls.

In the milk, dip the balls of mac and cheese, then the flour, then the egg then finally bread crumbs.

Then place the mac & cheese balls in a single layer in your air fryer and fry for 8 to 10 minutes per batch at 390 degrees.

Nutrients:

Amount per serving

Calories: 236kcal

Protein: 9g

Carbohydrates: 34g

Fat: 7g

Chapter 04: Dinner

This chapter will help you to learn and try the various basic varieties of recipes that are used on the usual basis in the dinner timings regarding food cooked in an air fryer. It definitely consists of an infinite number of options to try regarding your particular flavor. All the recipes are given in detail with the particular nutrients as well as ingredients.

4.1 Air Fryer Paprika Chicken Wings:

Yield: 4 servings

Cooking time: 30 mins

Ingredients:

- 1½-2 Lbs Chicken Wings
- Salt/Pepper
- Drizzle of Oil
- 1/2 teaspoon Garlic Powder
- Nonstick Spray
- 2 teaspoons Smoked Paprika

Instructions:

Spray with nonstick the Air Fryer Basket.

Mix the chicken wings with a downpour of oil, paprika, salt, garlic powder, and pepper, in a large bowl.

Wings transfer to the air fryer basket.

Air fry for 28-30 minutes at 400 degrees F or until the chicken wings are fully cooked. After halfway through the cooking time, flip it.

Nutrients:

Amount per Serving

Protein 58g

Calories 1150kcl

Total fat 86g

Cholesterol 279mg

Carbohydrates 34g

4.2 Spicy Buttermilk Fried Chicken with Pepper Jelly Drizzle:

Cooking time: 40mins

Yield: 6 Servings

Ingredients:

- 1 us liquid quart buttermilk
- 3 tablespoon minced garlic
- 0.25 cup hot sauce
- 2 teaspoon celery salt

- 2.3 tablespoon ground black pepper
- 2.3 tablespoon salt, divided
- 1 pound chicken which is cut into 8 pieces
- 0.5 cup milk
- 4 Eggs
- 4 cup flour
- 1 tablespoon crushed red pepper
- 0.5 cup seeded& minced red bell pepper
- 0.75 cup cider vinegar
- 2 jalapeño peppers, sliced thinly
- 3.25 cup sugar
- 2 Fresno chilies, sliced thinly
- 1 pinch salt
- 1 clove garlic, minced

Instructions:

In a large bowl, mix together the hot sauce, buttermilk, garlic, 2 tablespoons of salt, celery salt, and 1 tablespoon of black pepper. Coat the chicken in buttermilk mixture in an even way. With the buttermilk mixture and chicken, cover the dish and refrigerate for one night.

Remove your chicken from the fridge and allow it to reach room temperature (1 hr.). Remove the chicken from buttermilk mixture and discard the marinade.

In a small bowl, combine the eggs and milk. In a separate shallow bowl, mix the flour, 1 2/3 tablespoons of salt, and 1 1/3 tablespoons of black pepper. In the flour mixture, dip the chicken and shake off the excess. Then in the egg mixture, dip the chicken. Finally, dip the chicken again into the mixture of flour.

With cooking spray, spray the Crisper Tray. Put the Crisper Tray with the chicken. Slide the Crisper Tray into the Shelf Position no. 2. Set the Airfry (400 ° F/205 ° C) setting. Adjust the cooking time to 35 minutes. To begin the cooking cycle, press the Start Button. Cook until the chicken's internal temperature reaches 165° F/74° C.

Give the pepper jelly a drizzle whilst the chicken is cooking. In a food processor or mixer, mix the crushed red pepper, bell pepper, and vinegar and blend for some seconds.

Move the mixture to a heavy-bottomed, medium-sized saucepan and apply the remaining ingredients to the drizzle of pepper jelly.

Switch the saucepan to the top of the stove and heat the jelly on high heat until it cannot be stirred down to a vigorous boil. Then, extract the jelly from the heat and keep it undisturbed to cool to room temperature. The pepper jelly drizzle may be used instantly or kept for up to 6 months in an airtight jar in the refrigerator.

Move it to a plate when the chicken is finished cooking and serve with pepper jelly drizzle.

Nutrients:

Amount per serving

Calories 799

Total fat 59g

Cholesterol 138mg

Carbohydrates 39g

Protein 29g

4.3 Crispy Air-Fried Shrimp Sliders:

Cooking time: 45 minutes

Yield: 6 sliders

Ingredients:

- 3/4 pound deveined, peeled, and chopped shrimp
- 1/4 cup finely chopped celery
- 1/4 cup finely chopped yellow onion
- 2 tablespoons minced red bell pepper
- 1 teaspoon Creole seasoning
- 1/2 large egg, beaten
- 1/8 teaspoon salt
- 1/2 teaspoon baking powder
- 1/8 teaspoon cayenne
- 2 tablespoons chopped flat leaf parsley
- 1/2 serrano pepper which is minced
- 2 tablespoons finely chopped green onion
- 8 tablespoons (1/2 cup) fresh dried breadcrumbs
- Slider buns
- Nonstick cooking spray
- Tartar sauce and/or hot sauce for serving

- Lettuce leaves and tomato slices for serving

Instructions:

Combine the shrimp, bell pepper, onion, and celery along with the beaten egg in a dish. Add salt, green onions, cayenne, parsley, 2 tablespoons of breadcrumbs, and baking powder to the Creole seasoning. Mix thoroughly. Cover and refrigerate for 2 hours the mixture.

Take the mixture from your refrigerator and portion it into 6 even sized patties using a 1/3-cup scale. For the remaining six tablespoons of breadcrumbs, softly dredge the patties, finely coating them on both sides.

The air fryer should be preheated to 400 degrees F and the timer should be set for 18 minutes. Using cooking spray to gently spray the baking tray and put the shrimp patties on the baking tray. With the cooking spray, spray the top of each patty gently.

Place the patties in the fryer and cook for 16 to 18 minutes, until golden and crispy.

Dress with tomato slices, lettuce, and tartar sauce.

Nutrients:

Amount per serving

Cholesterol 145.2mg

Calories 899kcl

Carbohydrates 106.1g

Protein 45.3g

Fat 34g

4.4 Rotisserie Chicken:

Cooking time: 1 hour

Yield: Serves 4 to 6

Ingredients:

- One 4-pound whole chicken, rinsed
- 1/4 cup Rustic Rub

Instructions:

Use 1/4 cup of Rustic Rub to rub the chicken.

Truss your chicken. Attach the Rotisserie Spit to one of the Rotisserie Forks and tighten the fork screws. Slide the chicken into the secured spit fork on the spit rod. Secure the chicken with the other Rotisserie Fork and the screws on the Rotisserie Spit.

Insert the chicken inside the Power Air Fryer 360 into the Rotisserie connection.

Rotate to the Rotisserie setting of the Program Selection Knob. Rotate the Knob of the Temperature Control and the Time Control Knob to 177 degrees C for 55 minutes. To begin the cooking period, click the Start/Pause Button.

The chicken is ready to eat when the temperature of the chicken internally hits 71 degrees C. Click the Cancel button and remove the Power AirFryer chicken.

Nutrients:

Amount per serving

Calories 155kcl

Total fat 10.9 g

Cholesterol 50.2 mg

Total carbohydrates 2.7 g

Protein 11.8 g

4.5 Southwest Cowboy Steak with Skillet Corn Sauce and Tortillas:

Cooking time: 50 minutes

Yield: 4 servings

Ingredients:

- 1 flank steak
- 1 tablespoon Emerilís Southwest Seasoning
- 2 tablespoons olive oil
- 1/4 cup chopped fresh cilantro
- 12 Homemade Tortillas
- 1 1/3 cups Skillet Corn Sauce
- 1/2 teaspoon salt

Instructions:

With the oil, rub the meat all over. With the Southwest Seasoning, sprinkle it and pack cilantro leaves around the steak. Allow 30 minutes to marinate. Prepare the Skillet Corn Sauce and keep it warm.

Prepare the Homemade Tortillas. Get the broiler preheated.

Preheat on the roast setting the Emeril Air Fryer 360 to 425o F.

Place the steak on the aluminum foil-lined crisper tray and sprinkle the top side uniformly with the salt. Put the crisper tray on rack position 2 and roast it for 5 to 7 minutes for medium-rare meat. Turn over the meat and roast for 5 to 7 more minutes. For 5 to 10 minutes, transfer steak to a cutting board and let it rest. For thin slices, slice it diagonally against the grain.

Finish the Homemade Tortillas 10 minutes before the steak is over.

To serve, on each of 4 dinner plates, spoon 1/3 cup of Skillet Corn Sauce.

Nutrients:

Amount per serving

Calories 267kcl

Carbohydrates 0g

Fat 11g

Protein 0g

4.6 Crab Meat Imperial:

Cooking time: 25 minutes

Yield: 4 servings

Ingredients:

- 1 tablespoon olive oil
- 2 tablespoons minced shallots
- 3/4 cup small diced yellow onions
- 1/4 cup small-diced red peppers
- 1/4 cup small-diced celery
- 1/4 cup small-diced yellow peppers
- 3/4 teaspoon salt
- 1 pound crab meat
- 1/4 teaspoon cayenne
- 1 tablespoon minced garlic
- 1/4 cup chopped green onions
- 2 tablespoons chopped parsley
- 1 cup homemade or prepared mayonnaise
- 1/4 teaspoon Tabasco
- 2 tablespoons Creole Mustard
- 1/4 cup dried fine bread crumbs
- 2 tablespoons chopped chives, garnish
- 1/2 tablespoon Creole seasoning

Instructions:

To 360 to 400 degrees F preheat the Emeril Air Fryer.

Heat the olive oil in a large saute pan. Add the onions, shallots, peppers, salt, celery, and cayenne when the pan is hot. Saute until the vegetables are wilted for 5 minutes. Mix in the crab meat, garlic, parsley, and green onions and sauté for 1 to 2 minutes. Remove from heat and cool for 30 minutes or so. Combine crab meat mixture with 3/4 of a cup of mayonnaise, mustard, and Tabasco in a mixing dish. Mix until integrated fully.

Spoon the mixture into a ramekin that is medium-sized. Stir together the bread crumbs, the leftover mayonnaise, and the Rustic Rub in a mixing cup. Using the bread crumb mixture spread the surface of the crab mixture. Slide the tray into the shelf position no. 2. At 400 degrees F, select the cooking setting and set cooking time to 6 minutes. Click the start button and then cook until it is bubbly and brown.

Nutrients:

Amount per serving

Calories 335kcl

Total Carbohydrate 20.9 g

Dietary Fiber 1.1 g

Protein 23.0 g

Fats 15.7 g

Cholesterol 113.9 mg

4.7 Giant Stuffed Burger:

Cooking time: 25mins

Yield: 4 Servings

Ingredients:

- 3-pound ground beef
- 1 tablespoon Creole seasoning
- 8-ounce bacon, chopped
- 1 teaspoon Sea Salt
- 1 cup shredded Monterey Jack
- 1 teaspoon ground black pepper
- 1 cup shredded cheddar
- 0.25 dill pickles and diced small
- 0.25 cup Red Onion which is Diced
- 2 (11 ounces) pizza doughs
- 2 tablespoon water
- 1 egg yolk
- 1 tablespoon sesame seeds

Instructions:

In a bowl, combine and mix the salt, ground beef, Creole seasoning, bacon, and black pepper. Break the beef in half then flatten it into a circular disc for each half.

Place the Monterey Jack, red onion, cheddar, and pickles on one side of one disc. Then, top and seal with the second burger disc.

On the countertop, put half of the pizza dough and top the dough with a burger. Place the majority of the pizza dough over your burger and cover it. To produce an egg wash, mix the egg yolk and water in the small bowl. Using the egg wash to clean the dough and scatter sesame seeds on top of the dough.

On a spring form pan, tart ring or pizza stone that suits the Power AirFryer put the burger on the bottom. Slide a Crisper Tray to place 5 or 6 on the Shelf Position. Put the Crisper Tray burger on it.

Select the setting for cooking (165 °C). Change the cooking time to 25 minutes. To begin the cooking period, click the Start Button.

Let the burger rest for 35-40mins when the cooking period is full until being served.

Nutrients:

Amount per serving

Calories 1228kcl

Fat 81g

Carbohydrates 26g

Protein 91g

4.8 Sunday Roast Beef with Gravy:

Cooking time: 1hour

Yield: 6 Servings

Ingredients:

- 0.5 teaspoon salt
- 1 tbsp. seasoning of Emeril's Essence Creole
- 0.5 tsp. black pepper grounded
- 3 tbsp. flour
- 0.5 sliced large onion
- 1 pound round bottom rump roast
- 3 tablespoon olive oil
- 3 thyme sprigs
- 2 cup of low in sodium beef broth
- 5 clove Garlic, smashed
- 3 tablespoon butter, softened

Instructions:

With Emeril's Essence seasoning, black pepper, and salt, season your roast on both sides.

Put on top of the stove a Dutch oven. Heat some olive oil on both sides, add the roast and tan. Then the roast is removed and the thyme, onion, and garlic are added. Place your roast on top then add your broth, and then bring it to a simmer.

Then slide your Pizza Rack into the Shelf Position no. 6. Place uncovered oven on the rack for the pizza. Choose the Setting of Roast option (1hour cooking time). Then set the temperature of cooking to 163 °C. To begin your cooking period, click the Start Button. Cook until it reaches the ideal doneness.

Move it to the splatter when the roast has stopped cooking. Remove the thyme and onions from the oven using a slotted spoon.

In a shallow bowl, combine butter and the flour.

Move the roast to a pan. Remove the thyme and onions with a slotted spoon.

In a shallow bowl, combine the butter and flour.

Switch your oven to the top of the stove. Boil the drippings and then stir in the mixture of butter. To render the gravy, cook continuously until thickened (for 1 min.) when stirring.

To serve, slice your roast then pour gravy over your roast.

Nutrients:

Amount per serving

Calories 625kcl

Carbohydrates 0g

Protein 20g

Fats 0g

4.9 Baby Bam Burgers:

Cooking time: 20mins

Yield: 12 Servings

Ingredients:

- 1.5-pound Lean beef grounded
- 2 teaspoon minced garlic
- 0.5 cup of yellow onion chopped
- 2 tablespoon of ketchup
- 1 tablespoon Yellow Mustard
- 2 tablespoon of sweet relish pickle

- 1 tablespoon seasoning of Emeril's Creole
- 0.25 tsp. of black pepper grounded
- 0.5 teaspoon salt
- 12 hamburger buns (small)

Instructions:

Choose the atmosphere for the Air Fry (205 ° C for 18 minutes). Click and let your Power Air Fryer 360 preheat with the Start Press.

Use a wide mixing bowl to place the beef. Use your hands to combine the onion, salt, ketchup, garlic, relish, Creole seasoning, mustard, and black pepper so all of the products are well integrated.

Using around 1/4 cup for each, form the meat into patties. Place the Crisper Tray with the shaped patties.

Slide your Crisper Tray into the Shelf Position no. 2 as soon as the Power Air Fryer 360 is preheated.

Place the burgers in between buns when the cooking period is done and top with your favorite accompaniments, such as mustard, mayonnaise, slices of tomatoes, ketchup, pickles, onion slices, pickle relish, and lettuce.

Nutrients:

Amount per serving

Calories 10

Fats 0g

Protein 0g

Carbohydrates 2g

4.10 Pecan-Crusted Codfish:

Cooking time: 30mins

Yield: 4 Servings

Ingredients:

- 1 cup fried shoestring potatoes
- 0.25 cup olive oil
- 4-ounce cod fillets
- 1 cup roasted pecans
- 2 tablespoon brunoise red peppers
- 0.5 tablespoon seasoning of Emeril's Essence Creole, plus more for seasoning, divided
- 0.25 cup Breadcrumbs
- 2 tablespoon chopped scallions

Instructions:

To make fried shoestring potatoes:

To make shoestrings from 1 potato, use a mandolin.

Lightly toss in the vegetable oil the potatoes.

With cooking spray, spray the Crisper Tray. Place the Crisper Tray on the potatoes. Slide your Crisper Tray into the Shelf Position no. 2. Select Air fry setting. Set the temperature for cooking to 163 ° C and set the time for cooking to 10 minutes. To begin the cooking period, click the Start Button. When they are cooking, switch the potatoes regularly.

To foam Codfish Pecan-Crusted:

In a food processor, combine the breadcrumbs, roasted pecans, and Emeril's Essence seasoning. To form the pecan crust, purée the mixture until a mealy texture forms.

On the Crisper Tray, put the fillets and season fillets with the seasoning of Emeril's Essence. Slide your Crisper Tray into the Shelf Position no.2. Pick the setting for Airfry (205 ° C for 18 minutes). To begin the cooking period, click the Start Button. Flip the fillets after 4mins, and cover them with the pecan crust. Cook until fillets are properly cooked (about 12mins)

Move them to a plate when the fillets are finished cooking.

Nutrients:

Amount per serving

Calories 326

Fats 24g

Carbohydrates 15g

Protein 17g

4.11 Spicy Short Ribs Smothered with Red Gravy:

Cooking time: 8 hours

Yield: 5 Servings

Ingredients:

- 6-pound beef short ribs
- 1 pinch freshly ground black pepper
- 1 pinch salt, and more for seasoning
- 1 teaspoon liquid crab boil
- 12-ounce light beer
- 14-ounce ketchup
- 1 tablespoon molasses
- 1 tablespoon chopped garlic
- 1 tablespoon whole-grain mustard or Creole
- 0.5 cup chopped onions
- 1 dash hot pepper sauce
- 0.25 cup packed firmly light brown sugar
- 1 dash Worcestershire sauce
- 1 tablespoon grated & peeled fresh ginger
- 1 pinch ground cayenne pepper

Instructions:

Season the ribs with black pepper and salt. In a 4 1/2-quarter Dutch oven, put the ribs.

In a food processor, mix the crab boil, beef, ketchup, mustard, onions, garlic, brown sugar, Worcestershire sauce, hot pepper sauce, and ground cayenne, a pinch of cinnamon, ginger, and 1 pinch of black pepper. Process until it is completely smooth (about 15secs.). Scrape off the edges with a rubber spatula.

Pour over the ribs and fill the Dutch oven with the mixture. Slide the Pizza Rack into the Shelf Position no. 6. Place the Dutch oven on rack for the pizza. Select the Slow Cook (225° F/107° C) setting. Set the time for cooking to be 8 hours. To begin the cooking period, click the Start Button. Serve these ribs with the sauce when the cooking procedure is complete.

Nutrients:

Amount per serving

Carbohydrates 26.3g

Calories 1505kcl

Cholesterol 229.8mg

Protein 50.6g

Fat 128.7g

4. 12 Roasted Leg of Lamb:

Cooking time: 1 hour 30mins

Yield: 8 Servings

Ingredients:

- 2 tablespoon chopped fresh rosemary
- 1 tbsp. of seasoning of Emeril's Essence Creole
- 1 pound of boneless lamb leg
- 0.25 cup minced garlic
- 1 tablespoon of ground black pepper
- 2.5 tablespoon kosher salt
- 3 tbsp. freshly chopped oregano leaves
- 2 large yellow onions, quartered
- 2 bell peppers green that are sliced lengthwise into 1-inches strips
- 0.5-pound of carrots, cut & peeled diagonally in 1-inches pieces

- 3 russet potatoes of Idaho, quartered & peeled lengthwise
- 0.25 cup olive oil
- 0.5 cup of Chicken broth
- 0.25 tsp. of red pepper crushed
- 0.33 cup of squeezed lemon juice

Instructions:

Spread the seasoning of Emeril's Essence, 3 1/2 tablespoons of garlic, rosemary, 2 teaspoons of black pepper, 1 1/2 tablespoons of cinnamon, and 2 tablespoons of oregano onto the lamb. Position the lamb on the cutting board.

Roll your lamb with the butcher's twine and tie it. Stick the Rotisserie Spit to one of Rotisserie Forks and then tighten your fork screws. On the Spit, slide your lamb and into secured Fork. Use another fork and screws to protect the lamb with the spit. Insert Spit within the Power Air Fryer 360 through the Rotisserie ties.

Set the setting for the Rotisserie (190° C). Adjust the time of cooking to 70 minutes. To begin cooking period, click the Start Button. Cook before the lamb's internal temperature exceeds 57° C.

Put the onions, peppers, and carrots inside a big mixing bowl when the lamb has almost finished cooking. To mix, add 2 tablespoons of olive oil, 1/2 tablespoons of garlic and then toss. Add some potatoes, 1/2 tablespoon of garlic, and remaining olive oil to the mixture and toss.

Spread your potatoes, circling around to the other added vegetables, over the sides of baking pan.

In the separate dish, combine your broth with the lemon juice and pour your mixture on the potatoes and then sprinkle the red pepper that is crushed with all the vegetables, 1 tablespoon of black pepper, 1 tablespoon of cinnamon, and 2 tablespoons of oregano.

When you have finished cooking the lamb, cut it, and then reserve it then slide into the Shelf Position no. 1 the Pizza Rack. Place the pizza rack on the top of baking plate. Set the setting for Air fry (205 ° C about 18 minutes.). To begin cooking period, click the Start Button. Cook until potatoes are soft.

In the large serving dish, place the potatoes and vegetables then slice your lamb, and then place your lamb on the top of potatoes and vegetables.

Nutrients:

Amount per serving

Calories 205

Carbohydrates 0g

Fats 9g

Protein 28g

4.13 Cornish Hens:

Cooking time: 30mins

Yield: 2 Servings

Ingredients:

- 2.5 tsp. seasoning of Emeril's Essence Creole
- 2 tablespoon olive oil
- 2.5-pounds hens (Cornish game)
- 1 tsp. of Kosher Salt
- 10 Sprigs thyme
- 1 lemon, halved

Instructions:

Rub some olive oil on the Cornish hens and season with salt and Creole seasoning. In every cavity of each hen, put half a lemon and 5 sprigs thyme. Tie your hen in order to pin the wings behind its back and bring the legs together and upward.

Attach the Rotisserie Spit to one of Rotisserie Forks and tighten the fork screws. Onto your Spit and onto your secured Fork, slide the hens. Use another fork and screws to hold the hens on Spit. Insert the Spit inside your Power Air Fryer 360 through the Rotisserie ties.

Set the setting for Rotisserie (30min cooking time) and set the temperature of cooking to 171° C. Push Start Button to start the cooking period. Cook before the hens' internal temperature exceeds 74 degrees C.

Nutrients:

Amount per serving

Calories 207.7kcl

Protein 24.2 g

Total Fat 10.9 g

4.14 Emeril's Stuffed Shrimp:

Cooking time: 20-25mins

Yield: 6 Servings

Ingredients:

- 0.25 cup of green bell peppers, minced
- 0.5 cup minced yellow onions
- 1 tbsp. of minced garlic
- 0.25 tsp. black pepper grounded
- 0. 1 tablespoon of butter
- 5 teaspoon salt
- 1.5 tsp. of hot sauce
- 3 tbsp. freshly lemon juice
- 1 tablespoon Worcestershire sauce
- 1 egg which is lightly beaten

- 0.25 cup plus 1 tablespoon chopped parsley (fresh)
- 0.25 cup mayonnaise
- 0.25 cup of minced celery
- 1.5 cup of butter crackers, crushed
- 2.5 teaspoon Creole seasoning
- 16 to 20 shrimp
- Lemon wedges, for serving
- 3 tbsp. of unsalted butter

Instructions:

Position a saute pan on top of the burner. Sauté your butter, bell peppers onions, and garlic over medium heat until tender (about 3 minutes).

Remove from the flame the pan then let your mixture cool down. When cooled, blend to finish the filling with salt, Creole seasoning, hot sauce, black pepper, Worcestershire sauce, egg, lemon juice, and mayonnaise, celery, parsley, and 1 1/4 cups of butter crackers.

Apart from tail and the 1st connecting shell section, peel the shrimp. Then, devein lengthwise the butterfly and shrimp. With the filling, stuff your shrimp, drizzle the butter onto the shrimp. Scatter the leftover crackers of butter over your shrimp.

Slide the Tray into the Shelf Position no. 2. Slide into the Shelf Position no. 1 the Pizza Rack. Place the pizza rack on the top of the backing plate. Divide your shrimp equally between crisper tray & the baking plate.

Select the setting for the Air Fry (205 ° C for 18 minutes). To begin your cooking period, click the Start Button.

When your shrimp are finished cooking, eat them with your lemon wedges.

Nutrients:

Amount per serving

Calories 180

Fat 7g

Cholesterols 70g

Carbohydrates 18g

Protein 11g

4.15 Steak Roulade:

Cooking time: 30mins

Yield: 4 Servings

Ingredients:

- 1 tablespoon olive oil
- 3 clove Garlic, sliced
- 4 cup spinach
- 1.5 cup roasted peppers
- 2-lb flank steak

- 0.5 teaspoon ground black pepper
- 2 teaspoon Sea Salt
- 9 slice Muenster cheese

Instructions:

Position a saute pan on top of the burner. In a saute pan, add the spinach, olive oil, and garlic and sauté until wilted (2mins.). Remove the garlic and spinach when done, and let it cool.

On a cutting board, put the flank steak. On the flank steak, rub the salt and black pepper and then layer the spinach, Muenster cheese, and roasted peppers on the flank steak. To create a roulade, roll and then tie the flank steak.

Connect the Rotisserie Spit to one of Rotisserie Forks and tighten the fork screws. Then slide the roulade into the secured spit fork on the spit rod. The screws and other Rotisserie Fork protect the roulade on Rotisserie Spit.

Rotate Program Selection Knob (190° C for 30mins.) to the Rotisserie setting. To begin the cooking period, click the Start/Pause Button.

Let the roulade rest for about 10 minutes until being served.

Nutrient:

Amount per serving

Calories 243.7

Protein 29.7 g

Dietary Fiber 0.1 g

Total Fat 9.0 g

4.16 Bourbon Rotisserie Pork Roast:

Cooking time: 1 hour

Yield: 6 Servings

Ingredients:

- 0.5 cup Honey
- 1 orange, zested
- 0.5 cup light brown sugar
- 4-pound pork loin roast
- 2 tablespoon fresh orange juice
- 0.5 teaspoon salt
- 0.25 cup bourbon
- 0.5 teaspoon ground black pepper

Instructions:

In a small bowl, combine the honey, orange zest and juice, sugar, salt, bourbon, and ground black pepper and blend.

Position the Spit Rotisserie through the roast of pork. With the Forks, secure the Spit.

Brush the marinade gently on the bacon.

Insert the Spit into the 360 Power Air Fryer. Choose the setting for the Rotisserie, decrease the temperature of cooking to 350 ° F/175 ° C, and raise the time of cooking to 1 hour. To begin the cooking period, click the Start/Pause Button every 15mins, baste the pork with marinade. When cooking the pork.

Measure the interior temperature of the pork using a meat thermometer. The pork is done until the internal temperature exceeds 70° C.

For 15mins, let the pork rest until being sliced.

Nutrients:

Amount per serving

Calories 75

Fats 19g

Protein 96g

Carbohydrates 28g

4.17 Air Fried Chicken Breast:

Cooking time:

Yield: 6-7 servings

Ingredients:

- 4 eggs
- 2, chicken breasts skinless boneless
- 2 cups of buttermilk
- 2 cups cornmeal yellow
- 2 cups white flour
- 1 oz smoked salt Applewood
- 1 tbsp powdered black pepper
- 1 oz seasoning old bay
- cooking spray

Instructions:

For an egg buttermilk wash, mix wet components in a container.

For breading, mix the dry components in a separate dish.

To bake, switch selection dial.

Place Pizza Rack inside the Air Fryer 360 place for Pizza, the second up from bottom rack position.

Switch to a temperature of 425° F.

Switch to 30 minutes on the Time Dial.

Click the button for START.

The pre-heating of the Air Fryer 360 would start.

When being pre-heated:

In egg buttermilk wash, dip every chicken breast. Fully cover every chicken breast with bread. Spray the cooking spray on all the chicken outside. Put the chicken on the crisper container then wait before it stops pre-heating.

Click Start/Pause key until pre-heating becomes done. Then switch the time dial-up to the complete 30 minutes you picked initially.

To collect the drippings, put a baking pan upon a pizza rack.

Position Crisper Container in Air Fryer 360 on the Air Fry rack stage. This is just over Pizza Rack top, the level of the rack.

Close and click Start/Pause key on the Control Air Fryer 360. The cook will begin this.

Give time for the cook to finish it.

Verify that the temperature of the chicken is at a minimum of 165° F.

Nutrients:

Amount per serving

Calories: 151kcal

Carbs: 5g

Fat: 7g

Protein: 17g

4.18 Air Fried Crispy Balsamic Brussels sprouts:

Cooking time: 20 minutes

Yield: 5 servings

Ingredients:

- ½ cup red onions sliced
- 1½-2 cups brussels sprouts fresh and halved
- 1 tbsp balsamic vinegar
- Salt & pepper as per taste
- 1 tbsp oil or spray

Instructions:

In a cup, incorporate Brussels sprouts & chopped red onions. Olive oil (or cooking oil spray) & balsamic vinegar are scattered inside.

Sprinkle, to taste, with salt and pepper. To layer uniformly, stir.

Spray a basket of the air fryer with oil.

Add onions & sprouts. And do not clutter the basket. For air fryer version, prepare in batches if appropriate.

Cook at 350 degrees for 5 minutes.

Open-air fryer & use tongs to shake or throw the vegetables.

For an extra 3-5 minutes, cook. Mine was mildly charred for 8 minutes but still soft. Just ten minutes later, mine was crisp. Each type of air fryer is cooked differently. In order to determine the optimum cooking period, use your discretion.

Before serving, cool.

Nutrients:

Amount per serving

Calories: 46kcal

Carbs: 4g

Fat: 3g

Protein: 1g

4.19 Air Fried Marinated Steak:

Cooking time: 15 minutes

Yield: 2 servings

Ingredients:

- 2 New York Butcher Box Strip Steaks
- 1 tbsp Seasoning McCormick's Montreal Steak
- 1 tbsp soy sauce low-sodium
- 1 tsp of liquid smoke
- ½ tbsp cocoa powder unsweetened
- Melted butter
- Salt & pepper as per taste

Instructions:

Drizzle soy sauce & liquid smoke over steak Butcher Box. This can be achieved inside Ziploc containers.

With seasonings, season steak.

Refrigerate, ideally overnight, for at minimum a couple of hours.

In an air fryer, put the steak. Get two steaks grilled at a time (if air fryer is the standard size). An extra grill pan, sheet shelf, or the regular air fryer container may be used.

Cook it at 370 degrees for 5 minutes. Open-air fryer after 5 minutes and check your steak. Based on the target thickness, cooking time can differ. Cook to 125 ° F for rare, 135 ° F for moderate-rare, 145 ° F for moderate, 155 ° F for mild, as well as 160 ° F for well cooked. Using the meat thermometer.

Remove steak then drizzle with the melted butter after taking it out from air-fryer.

Nutrients:

Amount per serving

Calories: 476kcal

Carbs: 1g

Fat: 28g

Protein: 49g

4.20 Air Fried Cilantro Marinated Chicken Thighs:

Cooking time: 20 minutes and marinate for 2 hours

Yield: 4 servings

Ingredients:

- 1 tsp olive oil
- 4 boneless chicken thighs
- ½ lime juiced
- 1 tsp Seasoning McCormick's
- 1 tsp liquid aminos or soy sauce
- 2 tbsp chopped cilantro fresh
- Salt & pepper as per taste

Instructions:

You may opt to marinate meat in advance, or before cooking, season the meat. You should marinate the chicken ahead of time for a minimum of 2 hours (up to overnight).

Drizzle chicken thighs with the lime juice, olive oil, and soy sauce on both sides.

To taste, flavor chicken with seasoning, pepper & salt. First, add the meat to a lockable plastic container then flip the chicken to cover equally with the seasonings.

In the bag, mix the cilantro. Marinate it overnight for 2 hours.

Put the chicken in a basket with an air fryer. As chicken is covered with olive oil, you shouldn't need to mist the container with oil, but if you wish, do so.

Simmer the chicken at 400 degrees for 10 minutes. Place the air fryer open and turn the chicken over. For an extra 10-12 minutes, cook.

The overall cooking period can vary since each type of air fryer cooks accordingly. To determine when the chicken has done cooking, use the meat thermometer. When it has hit a core temperature of about 165 degrees, chicken is prepared.

Open an air fryer and take the chicken out. Before serving, nice.

Another part of lime is kept to extract fresh juice in chicken for additional lime flavor.

Nutrients:

Amount per serving

Calories: 209kcal

Carbs: 1g

Fat: 15g

Protein: 18g

4.21 Air Fried Beef Taco Egg Rolls:

Cooking time: 40 minutes

Yield: 8 servings

Ingredients:

- 1 lb minced beef
- ½ cup onion chopped
- 16 wrappers egg roll
- 2 minced garlic cloves
- 8 oz black beans refried
- 16 oz diced chilies and tomatoes canned
- 1 cup Mexican shredded cheese
- oil spray
- ½ cup kernel corn whole

Taco Seasoning:

- 1 tsp cumin
- Salt & pepper as per taste
- 1 tbsp chili powder
- 1 tsp smoked paprika

Instructions:

Over medium flame, apply the minced beef to the skillet as well as the pepper, salt, & taco seasoning. When dividing beef into smaller bits, cook till browned.

Apply the sliced garlic and onions until the meat has begun to brown. Cook until it becomes fragrant with the onions.

Add the sliced tomatoes, chilies, beans, Mexican cheese, and corn. To guarantee the combination of the mixture, stir.

On a hard surface, place the egg roll sheets. Dip it in water with a cooking brush. Glaze all of the roll wrappers around the edges with a wet brush. This would soften the crust & make rolling smoother.

On all of the wrappers, fill 2 tbsp of mixture. Don't overstuff it. You might have to double cover each egg rolls according to the type of roll wrappers that you have.

Diagonally fold the wrappers to close. For the filling, push tightly on the areas and cup it to keep it in place. For triangles, fold on the left & right ends. In order to end, wrap the top layer over the surface. To damp the area and keep it in place, add the cooking brush.

Spray a basket of air fryer using cooking oil.

Place the rolls of the egg into the Air Fryer container. Using cooking oil to spray every egg roll.

Cook at 400 degrees for 8 minutes. Flip the rolls of an egg. Cook for an extra four minutes or till crisp and browned.

Nutrients:

Amount per serving

Calories: 348kcal

Carbs: 38g

Fat: 11g

Protein: 24g

4.22 Air Fried Catfish:

Cooking time: 20 minutes

Yield: 4 servings

Ingredients:

- 4 catfish fillets
- 1 tbsp parsley chopped optional
- 1 tbsp of olive oil
- ¼ cup Fish Fry Louisiana Coating

Instructions:

Pat the Dry Catfish.

Toss the fry fish seasoning on either side of every fillet. Make sure the seasoning is covered with the whole filet.

On top of every fillet, splash the olive oil.

Put a filet in basket of Air Fryer. Do not pile and clutter the basket with the fish. If required, cook in chunks. Close it and cook it at 400 ° for ten min.

Keep air fryer open and turn the fish over. For an extra 10 minutes, cook.

Open & toss the fish.

Heat for an extra 2-3 mins or till crisp.

Cover with parsley optional.

Nutrients:

Amount per serving

Calories: 208kcal

Carbs: 8g

Fat: 9g

Protein: 17g

4.23 Air Fried Crab Cakes:

Cooking time: 15 minutes

Yield: 4 servings

Ingredients:

- Cooking oil
- 1 tbsp Seasoning Old Bay
- 8 oz crab meat jumbo lump
- 1/3 cup crumbs
- ¼ cup diced green peppers
- ¼ cup diced red peppers
- 1 egg
- ½ lemon juiced
- ¼ cup of mayo
- 1 tsp flour

Instructions:

Spray a basket of air fryers with oil.

Except for the flour, combine all the ingredients well.

Shape 4 patties into the mixture. Brush each of the patties with a splash of flour.

Put the Air Fryer with the crab cakes aside. Spray with oil on the crab cakes.

Cook it at 370 degrees for 10 minutes.

Before serving, cool.

Nutrients:

Amount per serving

Calories: 160lcal

Carbs: 6g

Fat: 8g

Protein: 14g

4.24 Air Fried Watchers Mozzarella Cheese Sticks:

Cooking time: 26 minutes

Yield: 5 servings

Ingredients:

- 1 cup breadcrumbs Italian
- 10 pieces string mozzarella cheese
- 1 egg
- 1 cup of marinara sauce
- ½ cup of flour
- Salt & pepper as per taste

Instructions:

Using salt & pepper to flavor breadcrumbs.

Set up the workspace by applying to different bowls the bread crumbs, flour, & eggs.

Dip every cheese string into the flour, then the egg, then the breadcrumbs.

For one hour, ice the sticks so that they can harden. This will allow the cheese to retain the form of the stick before frying.

Before each application, season the Air Fryer container so that things do not attach. Using the cooking brush to glaze the container using coconut oil.

Switch the Air Fryer down to 400 degrees. To the fryer, add the sticks.

For 8 minutes, cook. Remove the container. Flip every stick. Tongs may be used, but be cautious not to tamper with the form. For an extra 8 minutes, cook.

Before extracting them from the container, enable sticks to chill for 5 minutes. Around the outside, a few sticks may spill cheese. Enable cooling for the sticks, and use the hands and adjust the shape.

Nutrients:

Amount per serving

Calories: 224kcal

Carbs: 19g

Fat: 7g

Protein: 17g

4.25 Air Fried Crispy Fish Sandwich:

Cooking time: 20 minutes

Yield: 2 servings

Ingredients:

- ½ tsp garlic powder
- 2 tbsp white flour
- ¼ tsp pepper
- 1 egg
- ¼ tsp salt
- 1 tbsp lemon juice fresh
- 10 oz cut in half cod fillets
- ½ tbsp mayo
- Tartar Sauce Primal Kitchen
- ½ cup panko crumbs
- 2 buns
- Cooking oil

Instructions:

Breading:

Setting a station for cooking. In a bowl wide enough to swamp the fish, apply the garlic powder, flour pepper and, salt and pepper.

In a separate bowl wide enough to swamp the fish, apply the lemon juice, mayo, and egg to it. The egg is pounded and the components are mixed.

Connect to a different bowl of panko crumbs. Hold a wet towel in the vicinity. Your palms are going to get trapped

In the flour, dip the fish, after that egg mix then breadcrumbs.

Air Frying:

Spray the basket of the air fryer with oil and put the fish in a container.

Spritz the surface of fish with oil.

Cook at 400 degrees for 8-10 minutes, until crisp & golden. Do this after 5 minutes if you want to flip fish and then proceed to fry till crisp and brown.

The white fish is very fragile and tender. Be cautious if you toss the fish and when extracting it from air fryer when holding it. To make things simpler, use a rubber spatula.

Nutrients:

Amount per serving

Calories: 494kcal

Carbs: 48g

Fat: 21g

Protein: 28g

4.26 Air Fried Cheese and Chicken Quesadillas:

Cooking time: 10 minutes

Yield: 4 servings

Ingredients:

- 4 tortilla shells soft
- 1 tsp chili powder
- 8-10 oz chicken cooked cubed or shredded
- 1 tsp cumin
- ¼ cup onion chopped
- 1 cup shredded cheese
- ¼ cup tomatoes chopped

Instructions:

Season chili powder & cumin with your shredded meat. You'll still have to flavor chicken with pepper and salt if you're not using a prepared rotisserie.

With the tortilla shell, fill the air fryer. In a basket, you don't have to use some oil because quesadilla doesn't adhere to the basket.

To the tortilla, add 1/2 cup of cheese.

In the following manner, incorporate the rest of the ingredients: the tomato, onions, and after that the chicken.

Cover with 1 tortilla in addition.

Cook it at 370 degrees for 3 minutes.

Place the air fryer open and turn the quesadilla over. Using a spatula to cut and put the quesadilla on a tray. On the pan, rotate it and add it again to the air fryer.

For an extra 3 minutes, cook. You ought to heat it well enough for it to melt the cheese. Cook them longer for delicious quesadillas.

Using the air fryer to cut the quesadilla. Cut and serve.

Nutrients:

Amount per serving

Calories: 317kcal

Carbs: 25g

Fat: 14g

Protein: 28g

4.27 Air Fryer Crab Fried Rice:

Cooking time: 30 minutes

Yield: 5 servings

Ingredients:

- 6 oz meat lump crab
- 2 packets Brown Rice Ready Rice cooked
- 2 scrambled eggs
- ½ chopped red onion
- 2 chopped green onions
- 3-4 minced garlic cloves
- 3 tbsp soy sauce low-sodium
- 1 tbsp sesame oil
- 1 tbsp fish sauce
- 1 tsp of sesame oil
- 1 tsp of chili powder
- 1 tsp of paprika
- 1 tbsp red flakes
- Cilantro
- Salt & pepper

Instructions:

Prep brown rice, then put it in the fridge. About 15-20 mins, the rice would need to cool. It may even be placed in the fridge until it is cold.

To the base of push-pan, apply 1 tsp sesame oil.

In a large cup, mix the red onions, cold rice, green onions, garlic, & chili flakes. Drizzle all over the leftover sesame oil and stir.

The mixture is applied to push pan. In Air Fryer, put the pan.

Set the Air Fryer to 375 degrees. For 15 minutes, cook.

Season the chili powder, paprika, pepper, and salt with the crab.

Have the push pan removed. With rice, combine the fish sauce, crab, & soy sauce. Blend thoroughly.

For an extra 5 minutes, cook.

Get the rice removed. Mix scrambled eggs in. Using cilantro to sprinkle.

Before serving, cool.

Nutrients:

Amount per serving

Calories: 268kcal

Carbs: 31g

Fat: 11g

Protein: 15g

4.28 Air Fried Fish Sticks:

Cooking time: 25 minutes

Yield: 4 servings

Ingredients:

- 1 lb cod fillets skinless
- 1 beaten egg
- ½ cup white flour
- Cooking oil
- ½ cup of breadcrumbs
- ½ tsp of paprika
- ½ tsp of salt
- ½ tsp seasoning lemon-pepper

Instructions:

Break the cod into strips of 1 inch or whatever amount you want. Dry Pat.

Spray a basket of air fryers with oil. You should use a spray bottle of gasoline.

To soak fish sticks together with seasonings, put crumbs in the bowl big enough.

Set a prep station with 3 different bowls wide enough to soak fish sticks with flour, beaten egg, & seasoned crumbs.

Dip the flour with the tuna, then the egg, then the crumbs. Hold a wet towel in the vicinity. Breading could get sticky, sometimes.

Put fish sticks inside the basket of an air fryer. Using vegetable oil to mist. Don't leave the fish stacked. If required, cook in lots.

Cook at 400 degrees for 5 minutes.

Place the basket open and turn the fish over. Using vegetable oil to mist. Cook for 5-7 more minutes or till crispy.

Nutrients:

Amount per serving

Calories: 200kcal

Carbs: 15g

Fat: 3g

Protein: 18g

4.29 Air Fried Thai Chili Chicken Wings:

Cooking time: 30 minutes

Yield: 2 servings

Ingredients:

- 1 lb drummettes of chicken wings
- McCormicks Seasoning as per taste
- ½ cup of flour
- 2 finely chopped green onions

- Cooking spray
- Sesame seeds for garnish
- For Marinade:
- 1 tsp ginger grated
- 3 tbsp soy sauce
- 1 tsp rice vinegar
- 1 tsp raw honey
- 1 tbsp Sriracha
- 1 tbsp sesame oil
- 1 tbsp lime juice fresh
- 3 minced garlic cloves

Instructions:

Chili Thai Marinade:

In a tub, combine all the ingredients and put them aside.

Air Frying:

Spray a basket of air fryer with oil.

In a bowl wide enough to soak the meat, flour mixture & meat seasoning.

Pat the dry chicken. Coat seasoned flour over each chicken wing.

Put any wing in the basket of an air fryer. Don't be stacked. If required, cook in batches. Over the surface of the meat, spray oil.

Air-fry at 400 degrees for 12 minutes.

Place the air fryer open and turn the chicken over. For an extra 4-5 minutes, cook.

Remove chicken from the basket of an air fryer. Glaze Thai marinade over each chicken slice.

Send the chicken back to Air Fryer. Process till the chicken becomes crispy and has achieved a core temperature around 165 degrees, for 6-8 minutes. Using a thermometer for meat.

Place the green onions & sesame seeds on top.

Nutrients:

Amount per serving

Calories: 202kcal

Carbs: 10g

Fat: 11g

Protein: 12g

4.30 Air Fryer Beef Empanadas:

Cooking time: 40 minutes

Yield: 12 empanadas

Ingredients:

- 12 wrappers thawed Goya Empanadas
- ½ cup onion chopped
- ½ lb minced beef
- 2 minced garlic cloves
- 1 egg
- 2 tsp water
- 1 cup Mexican blend shredded cheese
- Taco Seasoning:
- ½ tbsp chili powder
- ½ tsp onion powder
- ½ tsp cumin
- ½ tsp garlic powder
- Salt & pepper as per taste
- ½ tsp paprika

Instructions:

Empanadas:

On medium flame, heat a skillet. To the skillet, apply the onions and garlic. Cook till they're fragrant.

To the skillet, apply the ground beef. With seasonings, season the beef. Split the beef into tiny bits using a meat chopper. Cook beef until it's browned. Drain the fat from the excess. Stir in the sliced cheese and mix until the cheese is molten.

On a flat surface, put empanada wrappers. Dip it in water with a cooking brush. Glaze all of the other empanada wrappers around the edges with a wet brush. This would soften crust to make rolling smoother.

In each empanadas, load the minced beef paste into the middle. Per empanada, apply 1 tbsp of beef. Don't overstuff it. With a spoon, flatten out the beef mixture.

Close empanadas. Using a fork to secure the empanadas by making indents in the crust around the edges. Around the side of each one, press down the fork in the crust.

In a tiny cup, put an egg and whisk it together with 2 tsp of water.

Using a cooking brush to glaze the egg wash on the surface of every empanada.

Air Frying:

Spray basket of air fryer with oil or surface with parchment from the air fryer.

Put empanadas in the basket of an air fryer.

Fry for 8-10 min or till crisp, at 350 degrees.

Nutrients:

Amount per serving

Calories: 261kcal

Carbs: 31g

Fat: 10g

Protein: 11g

4.31 Air Fried Corn Dogs:

Cooking time: 30 minutes

Yield: 6 servings

Ingredients:

- ¾ cup cornmeal yellow
- 1½ tbsp sweetener
- ¾ cup white flour
- 1 ½ tsp baking powder
- 1 beaten egg
- ¼ tsp salt
- Cooking oil
- 1 cup of buttermilk
- 6 hot dogs
- 1 ½ tbsp butter melted
- 6 popsicle sticks

Instructions:

In a wide cup, incorporate the dry items (flour, cornmeal, sweetener baking powder, and salt) and mix.

Incorporate in wet ingredients (melted butter, beaten egg, & buttermilk). Stir.

To immerse the dogs, dump the batter in a broad drinking bowl.

Take hot dogs from wrapper and fully dry them. This will make the hot dogs adhere to the batter.

You will need to split hot dogs in two, based on height of the air fryer.

Thread the skewers into hot dogs. Push the stick through the hot dog roughly 3/4ths of the hot dog.

Cover the air fryer container using parchment paper for the air fryer.

Dip every hot dog in the glass into the batter to make sure each is covered.

Place hot dogs inside the basket of the parchment-lined air-fryer. Using a spoon to apply more batter to certain places where there are parts of hot dog which are without batter. When you have corn dogs in Air Fryer, this is simpler to do.

Must not clutter the basket of an air fryer. If required, cook in batches.

Using cooking oil to spray corn dogs

Fry hot dogs at 400 degrees about 8-12 mins, till golden brown.

Before serving, cool.

Nutrients:

Amount per serving

Calories: 331kcal

Carbs: 28g

Fat: 18g

Protein: 13g

4.32 Air Fryer Grilled Chicken Kebabs:

Cooking time: 20 minutes and marinate for 1 hour

Yield: 4 kebab skewers

Ingredients:

- 2 tbsp liquid aminos
- 16 oz chicken breasts skinless, 1" cubed
- 1 tbsp Chicken McCormick's Seasoning
- Salt & pepper as per taste
- 1 tsp BBQ Seasoning McCormick's
- oil spray
- ½ sliced green pepper
- ½ sliced yellow pepper
- ½ sliced red pepper
- ½ sliced zucchini
- 4-5 of grape tomatoes
- ¼ sliced red onion

Instructions:

Chicken marinating would be recommended but not needed. Put the chicken inside a sealable container or wide bowl with chicken seasoning, soy sauce, BBQ seasoning, and pepper & salt to taste, if you intend on marinating the chicken. Marinate in the refrigerator for at least one hour, before midnight.

Remove and thread the chicken onto a skewer. During this process, your hands can get really dirty. To clean your hands, you might like to have a cloth nearby.

Layer the onions, peppers, and zucchini, over the chicken. Top with the grape tomato over top of each skewer. It could be more challenging to get the tomato skewers to place into the air fryer. After the chicken and vegetables have stopped frying, you should still add a tomato.

Using cooking oil to coat the chicken and vegetables. This is optional and creates chicken that is juicy.

For quick cleaning, you should line the air fryer using parchment liners.

Place the skewers in the air-fryer basket on a grill shelf. Cook at 350 degrees for 10 minutes.

Open and rotate the skewers with the air fryer. Cook until the chicken hits an interior temperature around 165 ° f for an extra 7-10 minutes. Checking the interior of one of the bits of chicken with a meat thermometer

Nutrients:

Amount per serving

Calories: 136kcal

Carbs: 4g

Fat: 3g

Protein: 23g

4.33 Crispy Air Fried Bang Shrimp:

Cooking time: 30 minutes

Servings: 4

Ingredients:

- 1 lb deveined and peeled raw shrimp
- ½ cup white flour
- 1 egg white
- ¾ cup panko crumbs
- Cooking oil
- Chicken McCormick's Seasoning as per taste
- 1 tsp of paprika
- Salt & pepper as per taste
- Sauce:
- 2 tbsp of Sriracha
- 1/3 cup non-fat, plain Greek yogurt
- ¼ cup chili sauce sweet

Instructions:

Preheat around 400 degrees Air Fryer.

With seasonings, season shrimp.

In three different containers, put egg whites, flour, and panko crumbs.

Build a station for cooking. Toss the shrimp into the flour, after that egg whites and then crumbs of panko bread.

You may not have to drench shrimp when coating shrimp with egg whites. In order to hold more of the flour on the shrimp, do a gentle dab. You would like the white of the egg to cling to the crumbs.

With oil, brush the shrimp.

To Air Fryer, add the shrimp. Around 4 minutes, cook. Open the basket then flips to another side of the shrimp. Cook for 4 more minutes or till it is crunchy.

For Sauce, mix the components in a little cup. To blend, mix thoroughly.

Nutrients:

Amount per serving

Calories: 242kcal

Carbs: 32g

Fat: 1g

Protein: 37g

Chapter 05: Desserts and Breads

This chapter will introduce you to the vast and basic recipes containing a variety of ingredients, regarding air-fried or air baked desserts and breads. These Dessert and bread recipes are exclusively for those who are searching for healthy and clean food.

5.1 Brown Butter-Pecan Bread Pudding with Bourbon Sauce:

Cooking time: 1 hour, 15 minutes

Yield: 8 servings

Ingredients:

- 3 large eggs
- 1 cup heavy cream
- 1 cup whole milk
- 3/4 cup light brown sugar
- 1 1/2 teaspoons ground cinnamon
- 3 teaspoons vanilla extract
- 1/2 teaspoon ground nutmeg
- 7 tablespoons unsalted butter
- 1/2 teaspoon kosher salt
- 4 1/2 cups cut into 1/2-inch cubes, day-old bread
- 6 tablespoons chopped pecans
- 3 tablespoons raisins
- Bourbon sauce
- 1 1/2 cups whole milk
- 6 tablespoons heavy cream
- 6 tablespoons granulated sugar
- 2 tablespoons cornstarch
- 2 tablespoons bourbon
- 1/8 teaspoon salt

Instructions:

In a medium cup, whisk together the eggs, cream, milk, 2 teaspoons of vanilla, cinnamon, brown sugar, nutmeg, and kosher salt. Just put it on the side.

Over medium fire, put a small saucepan saute or pan on the stovetop. Stir in 6 tablespoons of butter and let it melt. When melted, add some pecans and cook until the butter smells like nuts, is crispy and the pecans are toasted, shaking the pan and stirring regularly. Remove and switch from the heat to a tiny heatproof bowl.

To a mixing dish, add the bread and the raisins. To mix, add pecan-butter mixture and the reserved mixture of eggs and stir. Place 30 minutes aside.

With the remaining tablespoon of butter, butter a shallow (1and half quart) casserole dish and then transfer the bread pudding mixture onto the casserole dish.

On the Emeril Lagasse Power AirFryer 360, slide your oven rack into shelf position no. 5 and put the casserole dish onto the rack. Choose the setting for baking (325 degrees F for 30 minutes). In order to begin the cooking period, click the start button. Cook until pudding, is rich golden brown and gently puffed. (Cover with a piece of aluminum foil if the pudding is too dark on top until it is done cooking.) Move the casserole dish onto a wire rack and enable it to cool for about 30 minutes.

Make the sauce as the bread pudding cools: Put a small saucepan over medium-high heat on the stovetop. Stir in the milk, cream, and sugar and bring to a simmer.

In a shallow bowl, mix the bourbon and cornstarch together. Stir in the simmering cream with the bourbon mixture and whisk until it is thick. Stir in the remaining vanilla and salt and serve warm.

Nutrients:

Amount per serving

Calories 331kcl

Protein 9g

Dietary fiber 1.4g

Fat 5.7g

5.2 Cinco Leches Cake:

Cooking time: 1 hour

Yield: 12 servings

Ingredients:

- 1 tablespoon unsalted butter
- 2 teaspoons baking powder
- 1 cup all-purpose flour
- 4 large egg whites
- 2 egg yolks
- 1 cup of sugar

- 1 teaspoon vanilla extract
- 2/3 cup evaporated milk
- 2 tablespoons and 2 teaspoons whole milk
- 2/3 cup coconut milk
- 2 teaspoons coconut rum
- 2/3 cup sweetened condensed milk
- Sweetened Whipped Cream

Instructions:

The air fryer should be preheated to 350o F.

Butter a 9x9" baking dish on the bottom and sides.

Whisk together the flour and the baking powder in a small bowl. Beat the egg whites in a big mixing bowl with an electric mixer so the whites produce soft peaks. Beat in the sugar steadily. Add the egg yolks one by one, beating with each addition to blend. Combine the vanilla and whole milk in a separate small bowl. In 3 additions, add the flour mixture, alternating with the milk in 2 additions,

Slide the Pizza Rack to Position 5 on the Shelf. Position the Pizza Rack with the casserole dish.

For 20 minutes, rotate the Program Selection Knob to the bake setting. To begin the cooking period, click the Start/Pause Button.

Lower the heat to 325 F after 20 minutes and proceed to cook until the color of the cake is golden brown and when you hit it the center of the cake springs up. Place the cake on a wire rack and remove it from the oven. Leave for 15 minutes to cool.

Combine the condensed sweetened milk, coconut milk, evaporated milk, and the rum in a medium bowl and whisk well to blend.

Use a skewer to poke holes all over the cake's top. Slowly add the mixture of milk over the cake, making it absorb the liquid before adding some more. Garnish the sweetened whipped cream with the cake and serve.

Nutrients:

Amount per serving

Calories 266

Fats 13.8g

Cholesterol 74g

Carbohydrates 31.1g

Protein 5.2g

5.3 White Chocolate Macadamia Bread Pudding:

Cooking time: 30-40mins

Yield: Serves 6

Ingredients:

For Caramel Sauce:

- 1 cup of sugar
- 1/4 cup water
- 1/4 cup plus 2 tablespoons unsalted butter, cut into pieces
- 1/4 teaspoon sea salt
- 2/3 cup heavy cream
- 1/2 teaspoon vanilla

For Bread pudding:

- 1 3/4 cups heavy cream
- 9 ounces white chocolate chips or chopped white chocolate
- 1 3/4 cups whole milk
- 4 large eggs
- 1 teaspoon vanilla extract
- 1/3 cup sugar
- 1/4 teaspoon salt
- 1/2 cup chopped toasted macadamia nuts
- 1/2 loaf (about 9 ounces) day-old French bread, torn into rough pieces
- Whipped cream, for serving
- 1/4 cup unsalted butter, melted

Instructions:

For Caramel Sauce:

Put a pot on top of the burner. On medium-high flame, put the sugar and water to a boil until it is amber-colored. Remove the pot from the heat and briefly let it cool.

Whisk the cream and butter into the caramel cautiously. Then, apply the vanilla and salt, and stir.

For Bread Pudding:

Position a wide pan on top of the burner. Add the milk and cream and over low heat, and bring to a bare simmer.

Add the chocolate chips and remove your saucepan from the heat. For 1-2 minutes, keep the saucepan undisturbed and then whisk until chocolate is thoroughly melted.

In a big bowl, add the eggs, sugar, vanilla, and salt, and whisk. Add the combination of chocolate and whisk until it's incorporated. For 15 minutes, soak the macadamia nuts and bread in the mixture.

Butter a round 1.5-quart baking dish. Spoon the mixture onto the bowl and drizzle over the mixture with the remaining butter.

Slide the Pizza Rack into the Shelf Position no. 5. Cover the dish securely with foil and put the dish on the pizza rack.

Then, rotate the Program Selection Knob to the bake setting. Rotate the Temperature Control Knob and the Time Control Knob to 168 degrees C for 1 hour. To begin the cooking period, click the Start/Pause Button. Uncover the bread pudding until the timer hits 15 minutes.

Remove the dish after the pudding has stopped cooking. Let it cool.

Nutrients:

Amount per serving

Calories 449.0kcl

Fats 23.0 g

Cholesterol 230.0 mg

Carbohydrates 50.0 g

Protein 12g

5.4 Lemon Poppy seed Cake:

Cooking time: 1 1/2 hours

Yield: 1 loaf, 6 to 8 servings

Ingredients:

- 3 tablespoons coconut milk
- 2 teaspoons vanilla extract
- 3 large eggs
- 1 1/2 cups sifted cake flour
- 3/4 teaspoon baking soda
- 3/4 cup sugar
- 1/4 teaspoon salt
- 3 tablespoons poppy seeds
- 12 tablespoons (1 1/2 sticks) softened, unsalted butter
- 1 tablespoon lemon zest

Instructions:

Set the Emeril Lagasse Air Fryer 360 to set the timer to 1 1/2 hours at 300 degrees F the bake setting.

Combine the eggs, coconut milk, and vanilla in a medium-size mixing bowl and whisk it well to combine. Mix the dry ingredients together in a different medium mixing bowl and whisk it to combine.

Add 1/2 of your coconut mixture and butter to the dry ingredients and mix at a low speed using an electric mixer. Increase the speed to medium and beat for one minute.

Scrape down sides of the bowl and along with the lemon zest and poppy seeds, gradually add the rest of the coconut mixture in two batches.

Spoon the batter into a standard loaf pan that is greased. Bake until the tester inserted in the middle comes out clean, about one hour and 15 minutes usually. If the cake starts browning too rapidly before it is done, cover loosely with foil.

Nutrients:

Amount per serving

Calories 270

Carbohydrates 63g

Protein 5g

Fats 23g

5.5 Air Fried Peanut Butter and Jelly Doughnuts:

Cooking time: 26 mins

Yield: 6 servings

Ingredients:

For the Doughnuts:

- 1 1/4 cups all-purpose flour
- 1/2 Teaspoon baking powder
- 1/3 cup sugar
- 1/2 teaspoon baking soda
- 1 Egg
- 3/4 teaspoon salt
- 1/2 cup buttermilk
- 2 Tablespoons unsalted butter, cooled and melted
- 1 teaspoon vanilla
- 1 Tablespoon melted butter to brush the tops

For the Glaze:

- 1/2 cup powdered sugar
- 2 Tablespoons peanut butter
- 2 Tablespoons milk
- Pinch of sea salt
- For the Filling:
- 1/2 cup strawberry or Blueberry jelly (not preserves)

Instructions:

Whisk together the baking soda, sugar, flour, baking powder, and salt in a large bowl.

Beat the egg, buttermilk, melted butter, and vanilla together in a separate dish.

In the center of the dry ingredients, make a well and add in the wet one. To mix, use a fork and then finish by stirring with a wide spoon, just until your flour is mixed.

On a well-floured surface, turn out the dough. Notice that initially, it will be very sticky. Till it falls together, works the dough quite slightly, and now pat it out to a thickness of 3/4.

Cut out dough circles using a 3 1/2" cutter and spray with molten butter. Cut out 2 inches of parchment paper pieces and put each dough round onto the paper and then into the air fryer. Depending on how much can fit into the fryer, work in batches.

Fry for 11 minutes at 350 degrees. Using a pastry bag or squeeze bottle, fill every doughnut with jelly.

Whisk together the ingredients for the glaze and drizzle over each donut.

Nutrients:

Amount per serving

Calories 758

Fats 68g

Cholesterol 3mg

Carbohydrates 35g

Protein 3g

5.6 Air Fried Buttermilk Biscuits:

Cooking time: 25 minutes

Yield: 6 biscuits

Ingredients:

- 1 1/4 cups all-purpose flour, and more for dusting
- 1/2 teaspoon baking powder
- 1/2 cup cake flour
- 1/4 teaspoon baking soda
- 1 teaspoon salt
- 1 teaspoon granulated sugar
- 6 tablespoons cut into cubes, cold unsalted butter
- 3/4 cup plus 2 tablespoons buttermilk

- 1 tablespoon melted butter
- Fruit preserves, for serving
- Butter, softened, for serving
- Honey, for serving

Instructions:

Sift into a medium-sized bowl the cake flour, all-purpose flour, baking soda, sugar, baking powder, and salt. Run the cubed butter in the flour with your fingers or the pastry cutter until the bits are pea-sized. Apply the buttermilk and stir before the milk and flour fall together to shape the dough, using your hands or the rubber spatula. Take care not to over-mix.

Dust a work surface gently with flour. Onto the work surface, turn the dough out. Press the dough into a half-inch disc around 8-inches in diameter with your hands. To cut out 6 dough rounds use a lightly floured 2 and a half-inch round cutter. When cutting the dough, make sure to push straight down, for a turning motion can keep the dough from rising.

Then arrange the biscuits and brush them with some melted butter on the crisper tray or the baking tray. Slide the tray into the Shelf Position no.2. At 400 degrees F, select the air fry setting and set the time for cooking to 12 minutes. Click the start button and cook for 10 to 12 minutes, until the biscuits are flaky and golden brown.

Use sugar, preserves, or honey to serve the biscuits.

Nutrients:

Amount per serving

Calories 219kcal

Carbohydrates 24g

Protein 5g

Fat 12g

Cholesterol 22mg

5.7 Scallion and Cheddar Biscuits:

Cooking time: 8-10mins

Yield: 6 Servings

Ingredients:

- 1.25 cup All-purpose flour
- 0.75 teaspoon Baking Powder
- 0.5 cupcake flour
- 0.25 teaspoon baking soda
- 0.75 teaspoon salt
- 1 teaspoon granulated sugar
- 0.25 cup unsalted butter
- 3 tablespoon chopped scallions
- 0.5 cup grated cheddar
- 0.75 cup plus 2 tbsp. buttermilk
- Softened butter
- 3 tablespoon butter

Instructions:

Sift into a medium-sized bowl the cake flour, sugar, all-purpose flour, baking soda, baking powder, and salt. Run the cubed butter in the flour with your fingers or the pastry cutter until the bits are pea-sized.

Add the scallions and cheddar and mix to combine. Apply the buttermilk and stir until the flour and milk come together to shape your dough, using your hands or the rubber spatula. Take care not to over-mix.

Brush a work surface gently with flour. Onto your work surface, turn the dough out. To push the dough into a 1/2 in.-thick disc about 8 in., use your hands. Use a 2 1/2-inch gently floured one circular cutter for taking out six rounds of dough. When cutting your dough, make sure to push straight down, as a turning motion can keep the rising of the dough.

Brush the baking pan gently with a touch of melted butter. .Then, place the biscuits on the Baking Pan in a single layer and brush your biscuits with 1 tablespoon of melted butter.

Slide your Pizza Rack into the Shelf Position no. 5. Place the pizza rack on top of the baking plate. Select the Air Fry (400°F/) setting. Adjust the cooking time to 8 minutes. To begin the cooking period, click the Start Button. Cook till they're golden brown.

With the softened butter, serve.

Nutrients:

Amount per serving

Calories 206.7kcl

Fats 11g

Carbohydrates 20.5g

Cholesterol 30.5g

Protein 6.6g

5.8 Cheddar Jalapeño Cornbread:

Cooking time: 30mins

Yield: 6 Servings

Ingredients:

- 1.5 cup all-purpose flour
- 1.5 tablespoon Baking Powder
- 1.5 cup yellow cornmeal
- 1.5 teaspoon salt

- 0.25 teaspoon ground cayenne pepper
- 1.5 cup whole milk
- 3 large eggs
- 1.5 tablespoon minced, seeds & stems removed green jalapeño
- 0.5 cup grated sharp cheddar
- 1.5 tablespoon minced, seeds & stems removed red jalapeño
- 1 tablespoon vegetable
- 0.5 tablespoon butter
- 0.33 cup vegetable oil plus
- 1.5 tablespoon Honey

Instructions:

In a large bowl, combine the ground cayenne pepper, cornmeal, flour, salt, and baking powder and stir. In a separate bowl, combine the eggs, jalapeños, milk, cheddar, and 1/4 cup of vegetable oil and whisk together. To the dry mixture, add the liquid mixture and stir to combine.

With the rest of the oil, grease an 8 x 8 baking dish. Into a baking pan, pour the batter.

Select the setting for cooking (165 ° C for 30 minutes). To begin the cooking cycle, press the Start Button. Let your Power Air Fryer 360 preheat. Then, slide the pizza rack into position 5 on the shelf.

Place the baking pan onto the pizza rack. Cook until it comes out clean and lightly browned with a toothpick inserted in the center.

Brush the butter and honey over the top of the cornbread, remove the baking pan from your oven and let it cool.

Nutrients:

Amount per serving

Calories 150

Fats 2.5g

Carbohydrates 27g

Fibers 1g

Protein 5g

5.9 Molten Chocolate Cakes:

Cooking time: 15-30mins

Yield: 6 Servings

Ingredients:

- 0.25 cup Heavy Cream
- 5 tablespoon unsalted butter, divided
- 8-ounce semi-sweet chocolate, chopped, divided
- 5 tablespoon sugar, divided
- 0.5 teaspoon Vanilla Extract
- 2 large eggs, separated, divided
- 1 pinch salt

- Powdered sugar, for serving
- 3 tablespoon all-purpose flour
- Whipped cream, for serving
- Raspberries
- Vanilla ice cream, for serving
- Mint leaves, for serving

Instructions:

For Ganache:

Put a saucepan on top of the burner. In the saucepan, put the cream to a simmer over a low flame.

In a little bowl, apply 2 oz of cocoa. Over the sugar, pour the milk, let sit for 2-3mins then whisk to mix.

When firm, chill the mixture and then mold it into six 1-inch balls. In the oven, reserve the ganache.

For cakes:

Butter six ramekins of 6 oz with 1 teaspoon. Each ramekin has butter in it. Pour 1 teaspoon sugar in every ramekin then turn to coat, and then tap out any excess sugar.

Melt 6 oz of chocolate and apply 4 tablespoons of butter to a bowl. Over simmering water, set the bowl and stir to mix. Enable the chocolate to cool slowly then add the vanilla, egg yolks, and flour and mix well.

In the bowl of the electric mixer, place the egg whites and whip until thick and foamy. Beat in 3 tablespoons of sugar gradually and continue to beat just until stiff peaks are formed.

Until combined, fold egg whites into chocolate mixture.

Divide the batter evenly between the ramekins prepared. Inside each ramekin, press a ganache ball and cover with your batter.

Slide your Pizza Rack into the Shelf Position no. 5. On a pizza rack, place the ramekins.

Select the setting for baking (165 °C). Adjust the time of cooking to 15 minutes. To begin your cooking cycle, press the Start Button. Bake until puffed and slightly firm, but not browned.

When you finish cooking the cakes, remove them, and let them rest for 3 minutes. Serve with whipped cream, and vanilla ice cream then top with raspberries, powdered sugar, and mint leaves.

Nutrients:

Amount per serving

Protein 12 g

Carbohydrates 155 g

Fat 59 g

Calories 1170kcl

5.10 Air Fried Garlic Bread:

Cooking time: 6 mins

Yield: 2 servings

Ingredients:

For frozen Garlic Bread:

- 1 loaf Frozen garlic bread

For homemade Garlic Bread:

- Half cup butter
- 1 loaf French bread cut in half
- 1/2 tsp garlic powder
- Quarter cup grated Parmesan cheese
- Half tsp sea salt
- Shredded mozzarella or provolone cheese optional

Instructions:

To prepare frozen Bread Garlic:

Preheat to 176° C the air fryer for 5 minutes.

Insert the opened garlic bread into the air fryer.

French Bread Garlic Bread is baked in the air for 6 minutes at 176° C.

And enjoy it.

To make Homemade French Garlic Bread:

Preheat to 176° C the air fryer for 5 minutes.

In a saucepan, heat the butter, salt, garlic powder, and parmesan cheese until they are melted and mixed.

On the opened French bread, spray the garlic butter loosely and then add the loaves half cut to your air fryer pan. If you want, add shredded cheese now.

Air-fry it for 6 minutes at 176° C.

And enjoy it.

Nutrients:

AMOUNT PER SERVING

Calories: 290

Total fat: 12g

Carbohydrates: 35g

Protein: 10g

5.11 Sweet Potato Pie in an Air Fryer:

Cooking time: 1 hour 20mins

Yield: 4 servings

Ingredients:

- 2 Teaspoon Unsalted butter, melted
- 1 large Sweet Potato and you can use 2 cups mashed potato
- Two Cups Cold Water
- 2 Eggs
- Half cup of evaporated milk
- 1 teaspoon vanilla extract
- Half teaspoon ginger, ground
- Half cup of Brown Sugar
- Half cup of sugar
- Quarter teaspoon cloves, ground
- 2 tsp's of Cinnamon
- 1 teaspoon Nutmeg
- Salt, quarter teaspoon
- Cooking Spray
- 1 Pie Crust, cold

Instructions:

Scrub clean the exterior of the Potato.

Add some water into the instant cooking pot.

Through the inner/cooking oven, put the trivet.

Put the Instant Pot with the Potato.

Place and close the seal on your Instant Pot cover.

Pressure Cook for 18 to 22 minutes at high pressure.

Allow the release naturally. Or you can wait 30 minutes until a fast release is tried.

Drop its skin and the potato is ground up.

For this recipe, put two cups of your sweet potato, mashed in a wide bowl, no remainder will be needed.

The molten butter is combined with the sweet potato, mashed.

In another bowl, put all of the dry ingredients and combine.

Pour your potato and butter mixture into the blended dry ingredients.

In a big bowl, apply the evaporated milk, vanilla extract and eggs to your mixture and blend smoothly, having no lumps.

Position your Rack on the Air Fryer 360 Bake level, second up from the lowest.

Switch to bake with the Option dial, without Air Fryer Fan. Setup the temperature to about 350° F. Setup the duration to 50 minutes.

In order to preheat your Power Air Fryer 360, click the Start Button.

Spray a 9" dish for pie with the cooking spray when preheating.

From the refrigerator, take the crust of pie and put it in the 9" pie dish.

Into the pie crust, add in your sweet potato filling pie mixture.

Click the Start or Pause button until the preheating is over and switch the timer again to a complete 50 minutes.

In the Power Air Fryer 360, put the dish for pie on the rack.

To start cooking, click the Start/Pause switch.

Push the Start or Pause button after the 1st 25 minutes and turn the pie. Cover the sides with foil if the edges appear brown. Close, then click the Pause or Start button and restart cooking.

At the end of the cook, make sure that a knife or toothpick comes out clean.

Until chilled, refrigerate. Make sure the refrigerator is completely cold in the bottom middle of the plate of pie. This will take 3 plus hours or so.

Nutrients:

Amount per serving

Calories: 181kcal

Carbohydrates: 14g

Protein: 2g

Fat: 14g

5.12 Air Fryer Strawberry Pop-Tarts:

Cooking time: 25 minutes

Yield: 6 servings

Ingredients:

- 2 refrigerated pie crusts
- 1/3 cup low-sugar strawberry preserves
- 1 teaspoon cornstarch
- 1 teaspoon sugar sprinkles
- Cooking oil
- 1 oz cream cheese
- Half cup non-fat, plain vanilla Greek yogurt
- 1 tablespoon sweetener

Instructions:

Lay the pie crust on a smooth working surface. You can use a cutting board made of bamboo, too.

Slice the 2 pie crusts in 6 rectangles using a pizza cutter or knife (3 from each pie crust). As you are going to fold it over to cover the pop tart, each should be reasonably long in length.

In a bowl, apply the preserves and cornstarch and combine properly.

Connect to the crust a tablespoon of the preserves. Place the preserves in the crust's upper area.

To close the pop tarts, fold each over.

To create horizontal and vertical lines around the sides, make imprints on each of the pop tarts using a fork.

In the Air Fryer, bring the pop tarts in place. Do not stack. If desired, cook in batches. Use vegetable oil to spray.

Cook for 10 minutes at 370 degrees. To make sure they're not too crisp for your taste, you might want to check the Pop-Tarts for around 8 minutes.

To make the frosting, mix the cream cheese, Greek yogurt, and sweetener in a dish.

Until removing them from your Air Fryer, allow the Pop-Tarts to cool. It's essential here. They do split if you do not cool them.

Remove the Air Fryer Pop-Tarts. Cover the frosting on each one. Sprinkle sprinkles of sugar all over.

Nutrients:

Serving: 1pop tart

Calories: 274kcal

Carbohydrates: 32g

Protein: 3g

Fat: 14g

5.13 Air Fryer Dessert Empanadas:

Cooking time: 25 minutes

Yield: 12 servings

Ingredients:

- 2 apple honey crisp
- 12 empanada wrappers thawed
- 2 tablespoons raw honey
- 1 teaspoon cinnamon
- 1 teaspoon vanilla extract
- 1/8 teaspoon nutmeg
- 1 teaspoon water
- Cooking oil
- 2 teaspoon cornstarch
- 1 egg beaten

Instructions:

On medium-high heat, put a saucepan. Apples, honey, nutmeg, cinnamon, and vanilla are all included. For 2-3 minutes, stir and cook until the apples are tender.

In a shallow bowl, combine the water and cornstarch. Stir and apply to the pan. Cook for about 30 seconds.

Until loading it on empanada wrappers, let the filling cool for at least five minutes.

On a flat surface, put the empanada wrappers. Dip it in water with a cooking brush. Glaze each of your empanada wrappers around the edges with a wet brush. This would soften the crust and then make rolling smoother.

On each one, apply the apple mixture. Per empanada, apply 1 tablespoon of apple mix. Don't overstuff it. With a spoon, flatten out the mixture.

Close your empanadas. Use a fork to seal your empanadas by making indents in the crust around the edges. Around the side of each one, press the fork down in the crust.

Spritz a basket of air fryers with cooking oil. To the Air Fryer basket, add the empanadas. Don't leave the empanadas stacked. If required, cook in batches.

Brush the top of every empanada with beaten egg and use a cooking brush.

Set the Air Fryer to 400 degrees. Cook until crisp, about 8-10 minutes.

Before serving, cool it.

Nutrients:

Serving: 1empanada

Calories: 164kcal

Carbohydrates: 28g

Protein: 3g

Fat: 5g

5.14 Air Fried Blueberry Muffins:

Cooking time: 25 minutes

Yield: 12 muffins

Ingredients:

- 1 and a half cups of all purpose or the white whole wheat flour
- Half cup brown sweetener
- 3/4 cup old-fashioned oats
- 1 tablespoon baking powder
- Half tsp of salt
- Half tsp cinnamon
- 1 cup milk
- 2 eggs

- Quarter cup melted unsalted butter
- 1 cup blueberries
- 2 teaspoons vanilla

Instructions:

In a wide mixing bowl, mix the flour, brown sweetener, salt, rolled oats, cinnamon, and baking powder together. Combine.

In a separate, medium-sized dish, combine the eggs, milk, vanilla, and butter. Using a plastic spoon, mix it.

In the mixing tub, add the ingredients which are dry and wet ingredients and stir.

Fold and stir in the blueberries.

Divide the batter into 12 muffin cups and add them to your air fryer. It is optional to spray the liners with oil. Generally, the muffins don't stick.

Put the air fryer at 350 degrees. Carefully monitor the muffins for enough cooking time, since each model can cook differently. It will take 11-15 minutes to cook the muffins. If it returns clean on sticking a toothpick into the center of a muffin the muffins have done baking.

Nutrients:

Serving: 1muffin

Protein: 3g

Calories: 121kcal

Fat: 5g

Carbohydrates: 13g

5.15 Air Fried Lemon Pound Cake:

Cooking time: 50 minutes

Yield: 6 slices

Ingredients:

- 1 and a half cups of all-purpose flour
- Half tsp salt
- 1 teaspoon baking powder
- Half cup softened, unsalted butter at room temperature
- 4 eggs
- 1 cup sweetener
- 1 tablespoon lemon zest
- 1 teaspoon vanilla extract

- 2 tablespoons fresh-squeezed lemon juice
- 2/3 cup sour cream or plain Greek yogurt

Instructions:

A 6 cup bundt pan can be buttered and floured, or use the Pam Baking Spray.

In a medium dish, mix the salt, flour, and baking powder together.

To a mixing cup, apply the sweetener and butter. Cream the butter using a hand mixer. Mix together until creamy.

Add 2 eggs and combine well with a hand blender. Add and combine the leftover eggs.

In a mixing bowl, add the lemon zest, dry flour mix, yogurt, lemon juice, and vanilla. Blend so there is a nice batter.

Pour in the bundt pan the batter.

Cover the bowl with foil. Fry for 15 minutes at 320 degrees.

Remove the foil by opening the air fryer. Air-fry it for an extra 15-20 minutes. Check the cake by adding a toothpick if it is done. Ensure that it comes back clean.

Allow 10 minutes for the cake to cool.

Place a cake stand on the bundt pan and, to release the cake, turn the bundt pan.

Nutrients:

Serving: 1slice

Calories: 171kcal

Protein: 9g

Carbohydrates: 23g

Fat: 4g

5.16 Air Fried Chocolate Chip Cookies:

Cooking time: 30 minutes

Yield: 10 cookies

Ingredients:

- 8 tablespoons butter softened
- 1/3 cup packed light brown sugar or any sweetener
- 1/3 cup granulated sugar or sweetener
- 1 large egg that must be at room temperature
- 1/8 teaspoon freshly squeezed lemon juice
- 1 teaspoon vanilla extract

- 1 cup flour
- Quarter cup rolled oats
- Half teaspoon baking soda
- Half teaspoon salt
- 1 and a half cups semi-sweet chocolate chips
- Optional sea salt for sprinkling
- Quarter teaspoon cinnamon
- Half cup chopped walnuts

Instructions:

Cream the sugar, brown sugar, and butter in a mixing bowl for around 2 minutes using a medium-speed stand or hand mixer.

Place the egg, vanilla, and lemon juice together. Use the blender and blend for 30 seconds at low heat. And then blend for a few minutes on medium or until light and fluffy.

Add the flour, baking soda, oats, cinnamon, and salt and combine for around 45 seconds with a low-speed mixer. Do not over-mix.

Roll in the walnuts and chocolate chips.

Cover the air fryer basket with parchment paper of the air fryer. Scoop the cookie dough (about 2 tablespoons) into balls and put them about 1 1/2 to 2 inches apart in the basket. Use damp hands to flatten the cookies at the tip.

Fry for 6-8 minutes at 300 degrees.

Remove the basket from the air fryer and allow your cookies to cool for 5 minutes before they are extracted from the basket.

For an additional 10 minutes, move the cookies to a wire rack to cool.

Nutrients:

Serving: 1cookie

Calories: 300kcal

Protein: 4g

Carbohydrates: 13g

Fat: 23g

5.17 Paleo Pumpkin Air Fried Muffins:

Cooking time: 17 mins

Yield: 12 servings

Ingredients:

- 1 cup Pumpkin Puree
- Half Cup Honey
- 1 Tsp Nutmeg
- 2 cups Gluten-Free Oats
- 2 Medium Eggs beaten
- 1 Tbsp Cocoa Nibs
- 1 Tsp Coconut Butter
- 1 Tbsp Vanilla Essence

Instructions:

In the blender, put all the ingredients and blend until they are smooth. In tiny muffin cases, put the muffin mix, spreading out the muffin mix over twelve separate ones.

Put in an air fryer and cook at 180c for 15 minutes.

When cool, serve.

Nutrients:

Amount per serving

Calories: 121kcal

Protein: 3g

Carbohydrates: 22g

Fat: 2g

Chapter 06: Snacks and Appetizers

All of the basic recipes for air-fried snacks, dressings, appetizers, and side dishes along with their particular ingredients and nutritional information are discussed in detail and depth in this chapter. It will guide you to the best.

6.1 Sicilian Style Air Fried Broccoli:

Cooking time: 30 minutes

Yield: 4 servings

Ingredients:

- 1 1/2 pounds trimmed broccoli florets
- 3 tablespoons olive oil and more for drizzling if desired
- 1/2 teaspoon fine sea salt and more to taste
- 1/2 medium onion, julienned
- 1/2 teaspoon crushed red pepper and more for garnishing
- 1 tablespoon minced garlic
- 1/4 cup chopped or sliced pitted Kalamata olives
- 1 tablespoon nonpareil capers, drained
- 2 anchovy fillets, finely chopped
- 1 lemon, juiced and zested
- 2 tablespoons grated Pecorino cheese or Parmesan, to garnish
- 1/3 cup golden raisins

Instructions:

Carry three-fourths of a large saucepan filled with water to boil over high heat. Add the florets of broccoli and cook for two minutes. Drain and move the broccoli to a wide bowl. Stir in olive oil, garlic, julienned onion, crushed red pepper, and 1/2 teaspoon salt. On the baking tray, put half of the broccoli and slip it into slot 5 of your Emeril Lagasse Power Air Fryer 360. Set the unit to 425 degrees F for roasting. Use 12 minutes to schedule the clock. Cook until the onion slices are softly golden and the broccoli is crisp and tender. To a wide bowl, move the broccoli and repeat this with the other broccoli.

To mix, add the olives, capers, anchovies, raisins, and 1 tablespoon of lemon juice and toss. If needed, taste and apply more salt and lemon juice. Garnish with lemon zest, parmesan, and cracked red pepper sprinkles. If needed, drizzle it with more olive oil.

Serve it warm.

Nutrients:

Amount per serving

Carbohydrates 10g

Calories 52

Fats 1g

Protein 4g

6.2 Blue Cheese-Stuffed Burgers:

Cooking time: 30mins

Yield: 4 servings

Ingredients:

- 2 pounds ground beef
- 1 teaspoon salt
- 2 tablespoons Worcestershire sauce
- 1/2 teaspoon ground black pepper
- 8 tablespoons blue crumbled cheese
- 4 slices bacon, chopped & cooked
- 1/4 cup butter, softened
- 8 slices tomato
- 4 slices red onion
- 4 brioche buns
- 4 Bibb lettuce leaves

Instructions:

In a bowl, mix together the ground beef, salt, Worcestershire sauce, and black pepper.

Divide four balls of the beef mixture and divide every ball in half.

On the table, press the meat down. With the bacon and also 2 teaspoons of blue cheese per sandwich, stuff half the meat and finish it with unstuffed meat. The sides of the burgers are sealed.

Slide into the Shelf Position no. 2 the Pizza Rack. Place the burgers on your pizza rack.

For 18 minutes, rotate the program selection knob to your Air Fry setting (about 205 degrees C). To begin the cooking period, click the Start/Pause Button.

When you have finished cooking the burgers, remove them from your pizza rack and put them aside.

Cut into Shelf Position1 the Pizza Rack. Butter your brioche buns and put them, buttered side up, on the pizza rack.

Rotate the program selection knob for 10 minutes to the broil's setting (205 degrees C). To begin the cooking period, click the Start/Pause button. Broil the buns until they're golden. Then with the meat, lettuce, tomatoes, and red onions cut the buns and arrange the burgers.

Nutrients:

Amount per serving

Carbohydrates 1.9g

Calories 316kcl

Fats 21g

Protein 28g

6.3 Mac & Cheese:

Cooking time: 3 hours

Yield: 4 to 6 servings

Ingredients:

- 1/2 pound grated Fontina cheese
- 1/4 pound grated Parmigiano-Reggiano cheese
- 1/4 pound grated provolone cheese
- 3 tablespoons butter
- 1 1/2 cups milk
- 12 ounces dried ditalini pasta
- One 8-ounce can evaporate milk
- 1/2 teaspoon ground black pepper
- 1 teaspoon kosher salt
- 1/2 cup panko breadcrumbs
- 2 tablespoons chopped parsley

Instructions:

In a big bowl, combine all of the cheeses and blend. Set aside 1/2 cup cheese mixture.

Butter a casserole dish of 4.5 quarts that slides into the Power Air Fryer 360. Apply the mixture of butter, unreserved cheese, evaporated milk, pasta, milk, salt, and black pepper.

Over the pasta mixture, scatter the parsley then reserved cheese mixture, and then finally panko breadcrumbs.

Slide your Pizza Rack into the Shelf Position no. 6. Place the dish with the casserole on the pizza rack.

Rotate to the Slow Cook setting of the Program Selection Knob. Rotate your Temperature Control Knob and then Time Control Knob to 135 degrees C for 3 hours. To begin the cooking period, click the Start/Pause Button.

Rotate the Program selection knob for 10 minutes to the broil setting (205 degrees C). To begin the cooking period, click the Start/Pause button.

Nutrients:

Amount per serving

Carbohydrates 26g

Calories 310

Fats 17g

Protein 14g

6.4 Baked Mushrooms Stuffed With Crabmeat Imperial:

Cooking time: 25 minutes

Yield: 6 to 8 servings

Ingredients:

- 1 cup mayonnaise
- 1 teaspoon fresh lemon juice
- 1 tablespoon Dijon mustard
- 1/2 teaspoon hot red pepper sauce
- 1/4 teaspoon salt
- 1/2 teaspoon Worcestershire sauce
- 1/8 teaspoon cayenne
- 1/4 cup finely chopped yellow or red bell peppers
- 1 tablespoon butter
- 1/4 cup finely chopped celery
- 2 tablespoons minced green onions
- 1/4 cup finely chopped red onions
- 1 teaspoon minced garlic
- 1 teaspoon minced fresh dill
- 1 tablespoon minced fresh parsley
- 1 pound lump crabmeat that is picked over to remove any cartilage
- Fresh chives, garnish
- 1/4 to 1/2 cup grated Parmesan
- With portobello mushrooms:
- 6 large portobello mushrooms, stems removed and wiped clean
- Salt and freshly ground black pepper
- 1/4 cup olive oil
- With cremini mushroom caps:
- 36 cremini mushrooms, stems removed and wiped clean

Instructions:

360 to 400 degrees F. Preheat the Emeril Lagasse Power Air Fryer.

Mix the mustard, mayonnaise, lemon juice, Worcestershire, pepper sauce, salt, and cayenne in a wide dish. Stir until combined properly and put aside.

Melt the butter in a medium skillet over medium to high flame. Add the celery, bell peppers, and red onions, and cook for around 2 minutes, stirring, until wilted. Add the garlic and green onions and cook for 30 seconds, stirring. Remove and allow cool from the heat. Once cool, apply the parsley and dill to your mayonnaise mixture and stir until mixed. Wrap the crabmeat softly in it.

Stuff every mushroom cap with around 1 tablespoon of crabmeat imperial mixture while using the cremini mushrooms. Place and sprinkle with the Parmesan cheese on the baking sheet. Bake until warmed and bubbly on top (8 to 10 minutes) on the shelf position no. 5.

If portobello mushrooms are being used, cut out the gills on the underside of the mushrooms with a paring knife and remove them. Gently oil both sides with olive oil and lightly apply salt and pepper to the coating. Put on a baking sheet and bake for around 10 minutes, until tender. Remove from the oven and split the imperial mixture of crabmeat among the mushroom caps when cool enough to handle, and sprinkle with cheese. Bake for 10 to 12 minutes, before the mixture is cooked up and bubbly on top.

Take it from the oven and put it on a plate.

Nutrients:

AMOUNT PER SERVING

CALORIES 56kcl

Total Fat 3.9g

Cholesterol 23mg

Total Carbohydrates 2.4g

6.5 Gougeres Stuffed with Ham Mousse:

Cooking time: 30 minutes

Yield: Nearly 4 dozen

Ingredients:

- 1 cup milk
- 1/2 teaspoon salt
- 4 tablespoons unsalted butter
- 1/4 teaspoon cayenne pepper
- 4 large eggs, at room temperature
- 1 cup all-purpose flour
- Ham Mousse
- 1 1/2 cups grated Gruyere

Instructions:

Preheat the oven to 400°F.

Bring the salt, butter, milk, and cayenne to a boil in a big heavy-bottomed sauce pan. Remove it from heat.

Then add flour all at once and stir briskly, about 1 minute, with a wooden spoon to blend in. Return the mixture to heat and stir until your batter thickens into a ball and comes together. Switch off the heat and add 1 egg at a time then stirring well after each one has been added. Stir until you have satiny dough. Stir in some cheese and blend until the dough is dense and much of the cheese is melted. Transfer to a bag of pastry fitted with a plain medium tip.

Pipe the dough onto the prepared sheets in tiny mounds. Bake in the oven or the Emeril's Power Air Fryer 360 until it is golden brown and then puffed about 3 times its original size, 20-25mins in the oven or 10-12 minutes in the shelf position no. 5 of the Power Air Fryer 360. In order to prevent them from deflating, do not open the door of the oven for the first 10-15 minutes.

Take it out of the oven and let it cool a bit.

Cut the top of each gougere with a paring knife, keeping it either partially fixed or removed. In the middle of each gouger, pipe about 1 and a half teaspoons of the mousse and replace the tops.

Place the gougeres filled with mousse on a plate.

Nutrients:

Amount per serving

Calories 63kcl

6.6 Garlicky Air Fried Shrimp:

Cooking time: 20 minutes

Yield: 4 servings

Ingredients:

- 2 pounds medium shrimp, deveined and peeled
- 1/2 teaspoon cayenne pepper
- 1/2 teaspoon kosher salt
- 2 tablespoons olive oil
- 2 tablespoons minced garlic
- 2 tablespoons butter
- 1/4 cup dry white wine
- 1 teaspoon lemon zest
- 1 teaspoon chopped and fresh rosemary
- 2 tablespoons heavy cream
- 1 teaspoon Worcestershire sauce

Instructions:

Toss the shrimp with cayenne, salt, and olive oil in a medium dish.

Add the garlic and butter into the barrel pan of the Emeril's Air Fryer set to 370 degrees F and cook for 3 minutes. Add the wine, lemon zest, cream, rosemary, and Worcestershire, and continue to cook for another 3-4 minutes at 370° F. Add the shrimp and proceed to cook for 5-7 minutes longer or until the shrimp is cooked and opaque.

With a slice of crusty bread, eat immediately.

Nutrients:

Amount per serving

Cholesterol 572mg

Calories 228kcl

Protein 46g

Fats 3g

Carbohydrates 1g

6.7 Fried Green Beans with Garlic Lime Dip:

Cooking time: 10mins

Yield: 2 Servings

Ingredients:

- 0.5 cup flour
- 1 cup plain breadcrumbs
- 2 Eggs
- 2 tablespoon blackening spice
- 1 cup mayonnaise
- 1 pound green beans
- 1 clove Garlic
- 2 tablespoon parsley
- Juice of 1/2 lime

Instructions:

Onto a small bowl, add the flour.

In another shallow bowl, beat the eggs.

Combine the ingredients for the breadcrumb mixture in a third small bowl.

Dredge green beans into the rice, then into the eggs, and then into the mixture of breadcrumbs.

On two Air Flow Racks, put the breaded green beans. Place your racks on the Power Air Fryer Oven's lower and middle shelves.

Set the cooking period to 10 minutes and click the Power Button then French Fries Button (about 400 °F). Halfway into cooking time rotate the racks (5mins.).

In a little bowl, combine your dip ingredients and combine them together.

Use the dip to serve the green beans.

Nutrients:

AMOUNT PER SERVING

CALORIES 123kcal

Protein 5g

Carbohydrates 15g

Fat 4g

6.8 Korean Beef Wraps:

Cooking time: 10mins

Yield: 4 Servings

Ingredients:

- 0.25 cup low sodium soy sauce
- 1 tablespoon dark brown sugar
- 2 tablespoon fresh orange juice
- 1 tablespoon red pepper flakes
- 1 tablespoon minced ginger
- 1 tablespoon minced garlic
- White parts of 1 bunch scallions
- 1 pound sirloin steak
- 2 teaspoon hot sesame oil
- 2 tablespoon toasted sesame seeds
- Kimchi
- Steamed white rice
- Romaine butter lettuce or lettuce hearts

Instructions:

In a medium-sized bowl, mix the orange juice, white scallions, soy sauce, brown sugar, garlic, ginger, red pepper flakes, and sesame oil and mix. Then, add the steak and cover it with a toss.

Marinate your steak in the refrigerator in a tub for at least 4 hours.

Move the steak to Crisper Tray & Baking Pan until the steak is finished marinating. Slide into Shelf Position no.1 of the pizza rack. Place the pizza rack on top of the baking pan. Slide your Crisper Tray into Position 2 on the Shelf. Set the Air Fry (400° F/205° C) setting. Change the cooking time to about 10 minutes. To begin the cooking period, click the Start Button.

If wanted, serve the kimchi, beef, rice, and miso paste covered in lettuce or your favorite side dishes from Korea.

Nutrients:

Amount per serving

Carbohydrates 53.4g

Calories 441kcl

Fats 15.4g

Protein 19.8g

6.9 Wild Mushroom and Manchego Pizza:

Cooking time: 30mins

Yield: 2 Servings

Ingredients:

- 0.5 pound wild mushrooms
- Salt
- 1 tablespoon olive oil
- Fresh ground pepper
- 0.25 cup store-bought roasted garlic white sauce
- 1 pound Semolina Pizza Dough
- 4 slice prosciutto, Spanish ham, or any other thinly sliced cured meat
- Truffle oil
- 4 slice Manchego cheese

Instructions:

In a size of medium bowl, add the mushrooms, salt, olive oil, and black pepper and mix. Then, scatter the mushrooms over the baking pan on a single sheet.

Slide into the Shelf Position no. 1 of the pizza rack. Place the pizza rack on top of the baking plate. Select the Airfry (400 ° F) setting. Adjust the time of cooking to about 10 minutes. To start the cooking period, click the Start Button. Stir the mixture after half time through the cooking (5mins.).

Remove and then reserve the mushrooms until the cooking period is done.

Break the dough into two separate parts. Dust a work surface gently with flour. On the work surface, turn the dough out and roll every piece into 8inches rounds.

Place on Crisper Tray one pizza. Spoon half the sauce uniformly over the dough's surface. Place half the roasted ham, mushrooms, and Manchego cheese on top of the sauce and drizzle truffle oil on top of the pizza.

Then slide your Crisper Tray into Position 5 on the Shelf. Select the setting for the pizza (375° F for 20 minutes.). To begin the cooking period, click the Start Button.

Slide your Crisper Tray into the Shelf Position no. 1 when the cooking period is full. Pick the setting for the pizza. Set the temperature for cooking to 400° F and set the time for cooking to 2 minutes. To begin the cooking period, click the Start Button. When you finish cooking the first pizza, repeat the cooking phase on the second pizza.

Nutrients:

Amount per serving

Calories 1130kcl

Protein 41g

Fats 55g

Carbohydrates 120g

Cholesterol 94mg

6.10 Pecan Crusted Chicken:

Cooking time: 15-20mins

Yield: 4 Servings

Ingredients:

- 1 cup pecan pieces
- 1 tablespoon plus 1 tsp Creole seasoning
- 0.5 cup Breadcrumbs
- 2 large eggs
- 2 pound skinless & boneless chicken breast, cubed
- 0.25 cup olive oil
- 0.5 cup mayonnaise
- 2 teaspoon Creole mustard
- 1 pinch ground cayenne pepper
- 2 teaspoon Honey
- 1 pinch salt

Instructions:

Combine the breadcrumbs, pecans, and 2 tsp. Season with Creole in a food processor's bowl and pulse it for 1 min. to mix.

In a small dish, dump the mixture into it.

In a bowl, beat together the olive oil, eggs, and the remaining Creole seasoning. Dip the chicken in the egg mixture one at a time and then dredge it in pecan mixture as you shake it to eliminate some excess.

Place on the Baking Pan & Crisper Tray the chicken. Slide into the Shelf Position no. 1 of the Pizza Rack. Place the pizza rack on top of the baking pan. Slide your Crisper Tray into Position 2 on the Shelf. Select Air Fry setting. Set the temperature for cooking to 182° C and set the time of cooking to 15 minutes. To begin the cooking period, click the Start Button. Slide Crisper Tray into the Shelf Position no. 5 halfway through cooking time (71/2mins.), and slide the Baking Pan or Pizza Rack into the Shelf Position 2.

Combine the ingredients of honey mustard dipping sauce in a bowl as the chicken cooks then whisk them to combine.

So when your chicken has finished cooking, gently season with the salt and then serve with your dipping sauce.

Nutrients:

Amount per serving

Fats 9.7g

Calories 259.2kcl

Cholesterol 55mg

Carbohydrates 16g

Protein 24.7g

6.11 Shrimp & Pork Vietnamese Egg Rolls:

Cooking time: 10mins

Yield: 3 Servings

Ingredients:

- 3 tablespoon sugar
- 0.33 cup Lime juice
- 0.5 cup of warm water
- 2 tablespoon fish sauce
- 2 tablespoon vegetable oil
- 1 tablespoon chopped finely
- 0.5-pound Chinese sausage
- 1 tablespoon chopped garlic
- 0.5 cup minced yellow onion
- 0.25-pound bok choy
- 1 tablespoon chile-garlic sauce
- 0.5-pound Medium shrimp
- 1 tablespoon chopped scallions
- 1 cup matchstick carrot strips
- 1 cup bean sprouts
- 1 cup packed cilantro leaves
- 24 spring roll wrappers
- 1 cup packed fresh mint leaves
- Canola Oil

Instructions:

In a bowl, mix the sugar & warm water and allow the sugar to dissolve. To make the nuoc cham, combine the fish sauce, lime juice, and Thai chili. Reserve the Nuoc Cham.

Place the wok or a broad saut. Pan on top of the stove. Over a medium-high flame, heat the vegetable oil. Connect the sausage and stir-fry for 3mins when the oil is hot. Then add the garlic and yellow onion and cook for 2 minutes. Finally, add the shrimp and bok choy and fry for 1 minute.

Season it with garlic sauce and 3 teaspoons of cham nuoc. Reserve the remainder of the cham nuoc.

Remove the heat from the wok/sauté pan and let cool fully. Then, stir the scallion with it.

Dress lightly with nuoc cham and mix the bean sprouts, cilantro, carrots, and mint. Set aside the salad and the remainder of the Nuoc Cham.

Spread the bottom 1/4 of every spring roll wrapper with 2 tablespoons of shrimp mixture. Fold two sides into the middle of the wrapper and then stretch like a jelly roll, pulling together the edges to close. Repeat before binding is completed on all 24 rolls. Use canola oil to brush the egg rolls. Between the Crisper Tray and Baking Sheet split the egg rolls equally. Slide into Shelf Position no. 1 of the Pizza Rack. Place the pizza rack on top of the baking plate. Slide your Crisper Tray into Position 2 on the Shelf. Select your Airfry setting. Set the temperature for cooking to 380° F and adjusted the cooking period to 7 minutes. To begin the cooking period, click the Start Button.

Remove the egg rolls when the cooking period is done, then wash them on paper towels and repeat until the egg rolls have all been baked.

Nutrients:

Amount per serving

Calories 113kcl

Fats 6g

Carbohydrates 9g

Protein 5g

6.12 Bacon Wrapped Asparagus:

Cooking time: 15mins

Yield: 2 Servings

Ingredients:

- 10 fresh asparagus spears
- 5 bacon strips
- 0.125 teaspoon ground black pepper

Instructions:

Place asparagus on a waxed paper cover. Wrap around each spear a strip of bacon. Sprinkle the black pepper with the asparagus and turn to cover it. Using toothpicks hold the bacon.

Place in the Crisper Tray the asparagus. Slide your Crisper Tray into the shelf position no. 4. Set to Air Fry the Power Air Fryer 360. Set the temperature for cooking to 400° F and set the time for cooking to 15 minutes. Cook that asparagus until bacon is crisp (12–15mins).

Before serving, discard the toothpicks.

Nutrients:

Amount per serving

Calories 109kcl

Carbohydrates 3.7g

Fats 8g

Protein 6.6g

6.13 Mini Pizzas with Hot Italian Sausage:

Cooking time: 30mins

Yield: 4 Servings

Ingredients:

- 1 pound Pizza Dough
- 1.5-pound hot Italian sausage
- 3.5 cup tomato sauce
- Extra Virgin Olive Oil
- 8-ounce mozzarella
- 0.5 teaspoon crushed red pepper
- 2 tablespoon chopped fresh thyme leaves
- 0.25 cup Finely grated Parmigiano-Reggiano

Instructions:

Divide into four equal parts of the dough. Dust a work surface gently with flour. On the work surface, turn the dough out and roll each dough part into an 8 inches round.

Place on the Crisper Tray the sausage. Slide your Crisper Tray into Position 2 on the Shelf. Select the Air Fry (205° C) setting. Adjust the cooking time to about 15 minutes. To begin the cooking period, click the Start Button.

Shift one part of the dough into the Crisper Tray. One-fourth of the tomato sauce can be spooned uniformly over the dough. Sprinkle uniformly over the sauce with one-quarter of mozzarella. Put one-fourth of the sausage on top of the mozzarella. Add the crushed red pepper, thyme, and Parmigiano-Reggiano to the garnish.

Slide your Crisper Tray into the Position 2 on the Shelf. Choose a setting for pizza (20-min. cooking time). Set the temperature of cooking to 425 ° F/218 ° C. To begin the cooking period, click the Start Button. Repeat the cooking phase with the remaining pizzas when the 1st pizza is finished cooking.

Nutrients:

Amount per serving

Protein 2g

Carbohydrates 0g

Fats 2g

Calories 25kcl

6.14 Kicked-Up Tuna Melts:

Cooking time: 12mins

Yield: 4 Servings

Ingredients:

- 2-ounce cans solid white tuna which is packed in water, drained
- 0.33 cup chopped red onion
- 0.5 cup mayonnaise
- 1.5 tablespoon fresh lemon juice
- 0.5 teaspoon fine sea salt
- 0.25 teaspoon dried Italian herbs
- 1 teaspoon ground black pepper
- 10 thin tomato slices
- 10 ciabatta bread slices (1/2 inch thick)
- 10-ounce provolone cheese, sliced
- Potato chips
- Mixed green

Instructions:

In a bowl, mix together the tuna, onion, mayonnaise, lemon juice, salt, herbs, and black pepper.

On the bread slices, spoon the tuna equally and put the bread on your Crisper Tray. Place the tomatoes on top of the tuna and then Provolone cheese.

Then slide your Crisper Tray into the shelf position no.2. Select the Air Fry (400° F/205° C) setting. Adjust the time of cooking to about 12 minutes. To begin the cooking period, click the Start Button.

Take out the tuna melts when the cooking period is done, and then eat with potato chips or mixed greens.

Nutrients:

Amount per serving

Protein 48g

Fats 13g

Carbohydrates 7.9g

Calories 358kcl

6.15 Dehydrated Onions:

Cooking time: 10 hours

Yield: 4 Servings

Ingredients:

2 white onions sliced and 1/4 in. thick

Instructions:

Separate into circles the onions.

Slide your Crisper Tray into the shelf position no. 2. Slide your Pizza Rack into the shelf position no. 5. Place on the Crisper Tray & Pizza Rack the onion rings.

Rotate the program selection knob (49° C) to the dehydrate setting. Rotate to 10 hours with the Time Control Knob. To begin the cooking period, click the Start or Pause Button. Cook until they're crisp.

Nutrients:

Amount per serving

Calories 349kcl

Protein 9g

Carbohydrates 83g

Fats 0.5g

6.16 Garlicky Air Fried Shrimp:

Cooking time: 20 minutes

Yield: 4 servings

Ingredients:

- ½ tsp kosher salt
- 2 lb deveined & peeled medium shrimp
- ½ tsp cayenne pepper
- 2 tbsp butter
- 2 tbsp olive oil
- 2 tbsp minced garlic
- 2 tbsp heavy cream
- ¼ cup white wine dry
- 1 tsp lemon zest
- 1 tsp fresh rosemary chopped
- 1 tsp Worcestershire sauce

Instructions:

Stir the shrimp containing salt, cayenne, & olive oil in a medium dish.

Add butter & garlic into the barrel pot of Emeril's 5.3 qt. Air Fryer adjusted to 370 F and cook about 3 minutes. Connect the wine, milk, lemon zest, rosemary, and Worcestershire and proceed to cook for the next approximately 3 minutes at 370o F. attach the shrimp and proceed to cook for 5 - 8 extra minutes, or until shrimp is cooked and opaque.

With a slice of crusty bread, eat promptly.

Put wings in the Emeril's Air Cooker basket and set them for 22 minutes at 400° F. Cook until the wings are nicely browned, crunchy, plus thermometer measures at minimum 165 degrees F, rotating wings once in the center to encourage even browning. Move the wings to the container & spoon over hot wings with around 1/2 cup of sauce. Toss to cover equally and eat with hot wings.

Nutrients:

Amount per serving

Calories: 227kcal

Carbs: 12g

Fat: 11gm

Protein: 20g

6.17 Air Fried Crispy Brussels sprouts with Lemon, Garlic, and Parmesan:

Cooking time: 30 minutes

Yield: 4 to 6 servings

Ingredients:

- 2 lb halved lengthwise & trimmed Brussels sprouts
- 1 tsp kosher salt
- 3 tbsp olive oil
- ½ tsp red pepper crushed
- 3 tbsp Parmesan cheese finely grated
- 1 tsp minced garlic
- 2 oz sliced thick-cut bacon, ½" lengths
- ½ lemon finely zested

Instructions:

Along with olive oil, pepper, and salt, add Brussels sprouts in the wide bowl. Toss to cover equally, then move to Emeril 5.3-qt Digital air fryer's basket. Place the bacon pieces uniformly over the surface of Brussels sprouts, put the container in the fryer and cook at 400 degrees F for 10 minutes, or until bacon starts to crunch.

Remove the air fryer basket and stir sprouts properly. Decrease the heat to 380 & proceed to cook until crunchy and browned around the edges for 10 – 15 mins longer, mixing after five min to encourage even browning. Put the sprouts in a pot, stir in the lemon zest, garlic, & parmesan cheese, & serve warm or hot.

Nutrients:

Amount per serving

Calories: 79kcal

Carbs: 8g

Fat: 3g

Protein: 5g

6.18 Air Fried Mini Corn dogs:

Cooking time: 8 mins

Yield: 1 serving

Ingredients:

- 1 serving of Frozen Corndogs

Instructions:

Preheat the air fryer about 360 degrees F

Put the mini-corndogs at the base of the air fryer in the single layer. It would let them prepare unevenly by adding over one layer, and you will have a few undercooked corn-dogs.

Fry for 4 minutes at 360° F. Shake basket then fry for an extra 4 minutes in the cold. Whether you like a crispier small corn dog or whether your air fryer tends to undercook, add a minute.

Nutrients:

Amount per serving

Calories: 166kcal

Carbs: 15g

Fat: 3g

Protein: 8g

6.19 Air Fried Spaghetti Squash:

Cooking time: 30 mins

Yield: 4 servings

Ingredients:

- 1 suitable size for air fryer Spaghetti Squash
- 1 tsp of salt
- 1 tsp avocado oil
- ½ tsp of black pepper

Instructions:

Slice the spaghetti squash off the sides, and slice it longitudinally, making two pieces. Scoop out the plants.

Using oil to wash both halves and toss with pepper and salt.

Put both halves in your air-fryer basket with the sliced side up and cook for 25-30 min at 360 ° F.

Using a fork that fluff "spaghetti" midway through preparation, to allow uniform cooking.

Offer it as side dish or put it under gravy or tomato sauce as "spaghetti"

Nutrients:

Amount per serving

Calories: 50kcal

Carbs: 5g

Fat: 1g

Protein: 2g

6.20 Frozen Air Fried Chicken Nuggets:

Cooking time: 15 minutes

Yield: 20 servings

Ingredients:

- Chicken Nuggets Frozen

Instructions:

To bake, switch the selection dial.

Turn the knob to a temperature of 425° F.

Switch to 10 minutes on the Time Dial.

Air Fryer 360 can begin to preheat by pressing the Start/Pause Switch.

Put Chicken Nuggets over Crisper Tray.

Keep waiting until the preheating has ended.

Click the Start/Pause switch, then for the complete 10 minutes, turn the knob around.

Place your Crisper Tray in Air Fryer 360 at Air Fryer step, third from the bottom rack place.

To start cooking, click the Start/Pause switch.

Enable the cook to finish & enjoy it.

Nutrients:

Amount per serving

Calories: 90kcal

Carbs: 2g

Fat: 2g

Protein: 6g

6.21 Air Fried Roasted Asparagus:

Cooking time: 15 minutes

Yield: 4 servings

Ingredients:

- 1 bunch of fresh asparagus
- Salt & pepper as per taste
- Freshly wedged lemon optional
- 1 tbsp oil
- 1 ½ tsp seasoning Herbes-de-Provence optional

Instructions:

Rinse and cut rough ends of Asparagus.

Sprinkle the olive oil and seasonings with the asparagus. Cooking oil spray may also be used.

In an air fryer, substitute the asparagus.

Cook until crisp at 360 degrees for 6-10 minutes. Drizzle over roasted asparagus with freshly squeezed lemon.

Carefully check the asparagus, since each type of air fryer cooks uniquely. You'll want to see a slight touch of color on the cooked asparagus, but you certainly don't want this to be really slimy. You will burn it if you roast it for too long and it will get very sticky to the touch.

Start watching it closely after asparagus has heated for over 5 minutes.

Nutrients:

Amount per serving

Calories: 46kcal

Carbs: 1g

Fat: 3g

Protein: 2g

6.22 Air Fried Tortilla Chips:

Cooking time: 11 minutes

Yield: 48 chips

Ingredients:

- Kosher salt as per taste
- 6 tortillas
- oil spray

Instructions:

Using cooking oil to spray all faces of every tortilla (You can also spray them after they have been cut. Both methods work).

In 1 stack, position the tortillas. Using a pizza cutter or knife to split pile in two.

To make 4 bits, then flip the stack then cut again.

Then both vertically and horizontally, you'll slice down the center again to create 8 maximum chips per surface.

Toss salt all over the chips. If you like, you may incorporate some extra seasonings.

Load the air fryer with the chips. And do not clutter the basket. If required, cook in lots. Any chips which taste stale can result from overcrowding.

Fry chips at 370 degrees for 5 min.

Each type of air fryer can cook at various rates, so be careful to track your chips. Once they are nicely browned, firm, and also no longer supple & flexible, the chips are finally done processing. One chip may also be sampled to taste.

Nutrients:

Amount per serving

Calories: 112kcal

Carbs: 15g

Fat: 5g

Protein: 2g

6.23 Air Fried Zucchini Chips:

Cooking time: 25 minutes

Yield: 5 servings

Ingredients:

- 1 zucchini large
- 1 tsp Italian Seasoning
- ½ cup white flour
- 1 tsp Paprika
- Salt & pepper as per taste
- ¼ cup parmesan cheese finely shredded
- 2 beaten eggs
- oil spray
- 1½-2 cups of breadcrumbs

Instructions:

Spray a basket of air fryer using cooking oil.

Separate bowls by combining eggs, flour, & breadcrumbs.

Cut the zucchini to nearly 1/4 inch thick chips. For effective slicing, you may also use the mandolin. You ought to have the chips of zucchini all at the equal size so they cook at a temperature that is even.

Season flour with the pepper and salt and paprika per taste, then apply the shredded parmesan cheese.

In the flour, dip the zucchini, then the egg, and after that breadcrumbs then put them in the fryer. Making sure the chip is thoroughly covered in the eggs such that breadcrumbs adhere.

Since your palms will get sticky, hold a damp towel nearby.

Using the spray bottle to spray zucchini chips using oil spray.

Air Fry at 400 degrees for 5 minutes.

Open the chips and flip them. Sprinkle with extra oil and roast at 400 degrees for an extra 4-7 mins. Brown zucchini chips for 8 minutes, and if you want them crunchy, heat them a little too long.

Nutrients:

Amount per serving

Calories: 207kcal

Carbs: 31g

Fat: 4g

Protein: 9g

6.24 Air Fried Cream Cheese and Bacon Stuffed Jalapeno Poppers:

Cooking time: 15 minutes

Yield: 5 servings

Ingredients:

- 10 jalapenos fresh
- oil spray
- ¼ cup cheddar cheese shredded
- 6 oz of cream cheese
- 2 slices of crumbled & cooked bacon

Instructions:

To produce 2 halves of jalapeno, break each jalapeno in two, vertically.

Put it in a bowl with cream cheese. 15 seconds in the oven to soften.

Deseed the jalapeno from inside. (If you like hot poppers, save any of the seeds)

In a pot, mix together cream cheese, crushed bacon, & shredded cheese. Mix thoroughly.

For spicy poppers, apply a few of the seeds to your cheese mixture, as noted above, and blend well.

With your cheese mixture, fill each of the jalapenos.

Through the Air Fryer, fill the poppers. With cooking oil, brush the poppers.

Close Air Fryer. Cook poppers for 5 minutes at 370 degrees.

Remove and cool from Air Fryer prior to actually serving.

Nutrients:

Amount per serving

Calories: 62kcal

Carbs: 3g

Fat: 4g

Protein: 3g

6.25 Air Fried Crispy Crab Rangoon:

Cooking time: 30 minutes

Yield: 7 servings

Ingredients:

- 4-6 oz softened cream cheese
- 2 chopped green onions
- 4-6 oz crab meat lump
- Cooking oil
- 21 wrappers (wonton)
- 1 tsp Worcestershire sauce
- 2 minced garlic cloves
- Salt & pepper as per taste

Instructions:

By heating it for 20 seconds in the oven, you will melt the cream cheese.

In a little cup, mix together the green onions, cream cheese, Worcestershire sauce, crab meat, pepper, salt & garlic. To blend properly, stir.

Layout a working surface for the wonton wrappers. You may also use a large cutting board constructed of bamboo. With spray, wet each of the wrappers. Using a cooking tool to brush all of the sides with it.

Load per wrapper with around a tsp and a 1/2 of stuffing. Be alert not to overload.

Fold each wrapper to shape a triangle diagonally around it. Put the two opposing corners up against each other from there. Still don't close the wrapper. Bring the other two competing sides up, driving some air back. Squeeze together each of the sides.

Spritz a basket of air fryer with the cooking oil.

Load the Rangoon crab into the basket of the air fryer. Do not overfill or stack. If required, cook in batches.

Spritz oil with it.

Set the Air Fryer to 370 degrees. For 10 minutes, cook.

Open and flip the Rangoon Crab. Cook over an extra 2-5 minutes before they have hit the golden brown and crisp stage you like.

Take the crab Rangoon and eat with the dipping sauce you like from the air fryer.

Nutrients:

Amount per serving

Calories: 98kcal

Carbs: 12g

Fat: 3g

Protein: 7g

6.26 Air Fried Pizza Rolls:

Cooking time: 30 minutes

Yield: 32 pizza rolls

Ingredients:

- 1 tbsp olive oil
- ½ lb minced sausage
- 1 cup onions chopped
- 2 minced garlic cloves
- 2 cups of marinara sauce
- ½ cup of pepperoni
- 1 cup mozzarella cheese shredded
- Salt & pepper as per taste
- oil spray
- 1 tsp Italian Seasoning
- 64 wrappers, (wonton) double wrapping for pizza rolls

Instructions:

On medium-high fire, put a skillet and add the onions with the olive oil.

Cook till the onions become transparent and flavorsome, or for 2-3 minutes.

Using a meat chopper to apply the bacon, Italian seasoning, black pepper, and salt, & break this down. If the sausage isn't any pinker, cook about 3-4 minutes.

Pepperoni, marinara sauce, Garlic, and mozzarella are added. Lower the heat to medium and give 4-5 minutes to cook the mixture.

Set up the wonton wrappers on the dry cooking side. To damp the 4 sides of every Wonton wrapper, using water with the cooking brush.

For the filling, load each wrapper. Focus on the filling being filled to one side of the wrapper. It will make sealing simpler. In each one, using 3/4 of a tbsp of stuffing.

Seal the wrapper. To seal them to create a square, if you want to. To secure the closed side if appropriate, use a damp cooking brush.

Using oil spray to spray the rolls and position them in air fryer. And do not clutter the basket. It can take a longer cooking period if you pile pizza rolls, so each roll might not even cook at the same pace. Using parchment paper from the Air Fryer to make washing simpler.

Air fried the rolls at 370 degrees for 8 minutes. Get the rolls open and flip. For an extra 3-5 minutes, cook.

Nutrients:

Amount per serving

Calories: 211kcal

Carbs: 16g

Fat: 12g

Protein: 9g

6.27 Air Fried Wontons:

Cooking time: 25 minutes

Yield: 17 wontons

Ingredients:

- 2 finely chopped green onions
- 6 oz Softened cream cheese at ambient temperature
- 1 tsp sugar
- oil spray
- 17-21 wrappers (wonton)
- 1 tsp dried chives
- water bowl

Instructions:

In a medium dish, mix the green onions, cream cheese, sweetener, & chives. If you are creating wontons from pineapple, include the wontons here. Just stir well.

Take the wonton wrapper then dip the fingers in a little pan of water and then cover the 4 sides of wonton wrapper with your wet fingers. A cooking brush may be used, too. Based upon the manufacturer of the wonton wrappers which you choose, if they are incredibly thin, you might want to think double wrapping.

To the center of the wrapper, apply 1 tsp to 1 1/2 tsp of filling. The filling can spill from the wonton. Do not overfill. Smooth a spatula or spoon onto the filling.

To produce a triangle form, close the wrapper vertically. Ensure all the edges remain damp. This will hold it covered with the wrapper. You may fold them into a rectangular form as well.

In the air-fryer basket, spray the cooking oil. In a basket, fill the wontons and spritz them with gasoline. Don't clutter this basket of air fryers.

Water Fries at 370 degrees. For 8-10 minutes, cook. Each type of air fryer can cook at variable speeds. Check-in and cook the wontons to the ideal degree of crispness.

Nutrients:

Amount per serving

Calories: 46kcal

Carbs: 4g

Fat: 2g

Protein: 2g

6.28 Air Fried Tater Tots:

Cooking time: 45 minutes

Yield: 4 servings

Ingredients:

- 2 tsp white flour
- 1 ½ lb russet potatoes
- 1 tsp smoked paprika
- Salt & pepper as per taste
- 1 tsp garlic powder
- Cooking oil
- ¼ tsp thyme

Instructions:

To a simmer with a sprinkle of salt, put a saucepan or kettle ¾ of the way full of ice water. To fill the potatoes, apply ample water.

Add potatoes and leave about 6-12 mins to cook. You really should be capable of penetrating the potatoes on the outside quickly and know that the potatoes inside are firm.

From the water, take the potatoes. Clean them and make them cool off. Wait 10 minutes.

Using a wide area of the cheese grater then scrape the potatoes until cooled. Squeeze out the potatoes for some extra water.

Put grated potatoes and the flour & seasonings in a dish. Russet potatoes seem bland, in taste. Make sure to taste the salt. Stir to blend.

To shape tots with mixture, use your hands. If you wish, you may build even smaller or bigger tots.

Spray the tots as well with cooking oil on all ends. In an air fryer, put the tots. Air Fry at 400 degrees for 10 minutes.

Open the fryer in the air and rotate the tots. Process for another five min or until perfect crisp has been hit by the tots.

Nutrients:

Amount per serving

Calories: 70kcal

Carbs: 13g

Fat: 1g

Protein: 2g

6.29 Air Fried Cheese Stuffed Mushrooms:

Cooking time: 15 minutes

Yield: 5 servings

Ingredients:

- 8 oz fresh mushrooms large
- ¼ cup shredded parmesan cheese
- Salt & pepper as per taste
- 4 oz of cream cheese
- 1/8 cup cheddar cheese sharp shredded
- 1 tsp Worcestershire sauce
- 1/8 cup cheddar cheese white shredded
- 2 chopped garlic cloves

Instructions:

To prep, it for filling, take stem out of the mushroom. Chop the stem off first then create a circular-cut across the region where the stem is located. Keep chopping so you can extract the excess fungi.

For 15 seconds, put cream cheese in microwave to melt.

In a medium cup, combine all the grated cheeses, the cream cheese, pepper, salt, & Worcestershire sauce. Stir to blend.

With the cheese paste, stuff the mushrooms.

Let the mushrooms at 370 degrees in Air Fryer for about 8 minutes.

Until serving, enable mushrooms to settle.

Nutrients:

Amount per serving

Calories: 116kcal

Carbs: 3g

Fat: 8g

Protein: 8g

6.30 Air Fried Potato Wedges:

Cooking time: 25 minutes

Yield: 5 servings

Ingredients:

- 4 russet potatoes medium
- ½ tbsp seasoning Herbes-de-Provence
- 1 tbsp olive oil
- oil spray
- 1 tsp garlic powder
- Salt & pepper as per taste
- 1 tsp smoked paprika

Instructions:

Clean the potatoes very well and scrub them. Cut all potato lengthwise in half, then diagonally cut the potato to produce 8-10 slices per potato. Check to be sure their thickness & size are exactly the same.

In hot water Put sliced potatoes. This would minimize excessive starch & help to crisp the potatoes. For 20 to 30 minutes, leaving potatoes in a hot bath.

Using paper towels, extract potatoes from water then dry them.

In a big, dry tub, add the potatoes. Drizzle all over with the olive oil, then apply the seasonings. In order to make sure that potatoes are uniformly coated, flip with tongs.

Using oil spray to spray air fryer container. To the basket, apply potato wedges. If needed, do not overload the basket & cook in parts.

Cook at 400 degrees for twelve minutes.

Open-air fryer and then use tongs to turn the wedges. For an extra 10-15 min, cook.

Before serving, cool.

Nutrients:

Amount per serving

Calories: 115kcal

Carbs: 19g

Fat: 3g

Protein: 3g

6.31 Air Fried Cheesy Garlic Bread:

Cooking time: 20 minutes

Yield: 8 servings

Ingredients:

- 2 tbsp ghee or unsalted butter
- 1 tbsp parsley finely chopped
- 2 tbsp olive oil
- 1 cup mozzarella cheese shredded
- 1 tsp Italian Seasoning
- Salt & pepper as per taste
- 4 minced garlic cloves
- 1 bread loaf sourdough

Instructions:

Melt the butter for around 15-30 seconds in the microwave in a tiny tub.

Stir in the butter with olive oil, parsley, garlic, Italian seasoning, pepper, and salt.

Put the bread in a clear, horizontal position. Without slicing through bread, split the bread with a grooved bread knife vertically, around 2/3rds of way in through bread. Stop the bread's edges (about 1 inch from the corners). To produce little diamond forms, transform the bread around to make diagonal slits the other direction.

Through the crevices in the bread, fill garlic butter olive oil. Using a brush for cooking.

Next, in each of the holes, apply the cheese. It's possible to use shredded or cubed cheese. If you use sliced cheese, consider stuffing the cheese with a butter knife into the bread.

Put the bread in the frying pan. Cook for 5 minutes at 350 degrees, or until cheese is fully melted. Before serving, cool.

Nutrients:

Amount per serving

Calories: 325kcal

Carbs: 45g

Fat: 10g

Protein: 11g

6.32 Air Fried Crunchy Pickles:

Cooking time: 30 minutes

Yield: 6 servings

Ingredients:

- 24 oz sliced dill pickle
- 1 egg
- 1¾-2 cups of Panko breadcrumbs
- ¾ cup of flour
- ½ tbsp dried dill
- ¾ cup of buttermilk
- ½ tsp garlic powder
- oil spray
- Salt & pepper as per taste

Instructions:

Spritz air fryer container with the cooking oil.

Fully dry the pickles. This would render bread simpler for them.

To swamp the pickles, add flour to the bowl big enough. With garlic powder, dried dill, pepper, and salt to taste, season the flour.

Combine the prepared flour with the buttermilk & egg. Beat & stir to blend together.

To dig the pickles, put panko breadcrumbs in the separate bowl wide enough.

Submerge the pickles and afterward panko breadcrumbs in flour buttermilk combination. Keep ready for your hands with a wet kitchen towel. They're starting to be messy.

On a dish, put breaded pickles. Freeze pickles for fifteen min after breading pickles. It's optional, although strongly encouraged, move. It helps preserve the intact breading.

In an air fryer, put the pickles. Don't leave them stacked. If required, cook in batches.

In cooking oil, brush the pickles.

Cook at 400 degrees for 7-10 minutes, tossing after five min. Each brand of air fryer can cook at distinct speeds.

Combine fried pickles and dried dill finished with ranch.

Nutrients:

Amount per serving

Calories: 142kcal

Carbs: 29g

Fat: 2g

Protein: 6g

6.33 Air Fried Cornbread:

Cooking time: 25 minutes

Yield: 8 servings

Ingredients:

- 1 cup cornmeal mix self-rising
- ¼ cup of sugar
- ¼ tsp salt
- ¼ cup of unsalted butter & ½ melted stick
- ¾ cup of buttermilk
- 1 egg

Instructions:

To a mixing pot, apply the cornmeal, sweetener & salt. Stir to blend.

Then substitute the potato, the majority of the butter, and the buttermilk. Whisk to combine.

Be careful not to blend the batter too much. Over-mixing can cause the crust to crack heavily and crumble a lot. Only blend long enough for the components to combine.

In an air fryer, put the silicone baking tooling. Pour the mixture into one of the muffin molds constructed of silicone. Fill 3/4ths of each mold absolutely. You could have to prepare in batches, depending on the size of an air fryer.

Cook cornbread muffins at 330 degrees for 11-15 minutes. By putting a toothpick in the middle of a muffin, measure whether the cornbread has stopped and made sure your toothpick comes clean.

Nutrients:

Amount per serving

Calories: 123kcal

Carbs: 11g

Fat: 7g

Protein: 3g

6.34 Air Fried Croutons:

Cooking time: 13 minutes

Yield: 8 servings

Ingredients:

- 2 cups sourdough bread sliced
- ½ tbsp any seasoning
- 1 tbsp olive oil
- Onion Powder
- Salt & pepper as per taste
- Smoked Paprika
- Dried Rosemary

Instructions:

You would be using a ridged knife to split the bread if you are preparing the sourdough loaf.

Drizzle the bread with olive oil. Season with seasonings. Try a little extra oil if you notice that the seasonings don't stick.

Put sliced bread in the basket of an air fryer.

Air fry it at 370 degrees for around 5 minutes. Open the croutons then flip/shake them.

Air fry about 2-3 minutes more.

Nutrients:

Amount per serving

Calories: 85kcal

Carbs: 14g

Fat: 2g

Protein: 2g

6.35 Air Fried Beef Jerky:

Cooking time: 1 hour

Yield: 24 jerkies

Ingredients:

- 1 ½ lb steak sirloin tip
- 1 tsp Worcestershire sauce
- 1/3 cup of soy sauce
- ½ cup of brown sweetener
- 1 tsp smoked paprika
- 1 tsp liquid smoke
- 1 tsp garlic powder
- ½ tsp black pepper
- 1 tsp onion powder
- 1 tsp red pepper optional

Instructions:

Cut the steak about 1/8" wide into small strips. It's going to be chewier when you cut with the grain.

In a wide tub, substitute the steak. Put in all the marinade components and mix.

Chill in the fridge for a minimum of 30 min. The more you soak, then the more jerky would have more spice.

Beef jerkies could easily be put in an air fryer container. First, brush with olive oil. Do not pile the basket or clutter it. It can take longer to cook.

Air fried for 60 – 75 minutes at 180 degrees, if you string the beef around the skewers.

If you put beef in an air-fryer basket, fry it at 180 ° for around 2-3 hrs.

Watch the beef with all strategies to ensure it meets your ideal consistency.

The bamboo solution is typically the nearest to jerky.

Nutrients:

Amount per serving

Calories: 46kcal

Carbs: 1g

Fat: 2g

Protein: 6g

6.36 Crispy Air Fried Artichoke Hearts:

Cooking time: 20 minutes

Servings: 8

Ingredients:

- 2-3 cans dried & drained Quartered Artichokes
- 1 cup of panko breadcrumbs
- ½ cup of mayonnaise
- 1/3 cup Parmesan grated
- Sprinkle with parsley to garnish
- Salt & pepper as per taste

Instructions:

Drain the artichokes in the strainer.

Switch to a plate & put between paper towel layers & pat dry.

Add pepper, salt & mayo, to a small bowl and toss gently to cover.

In a zip-top container, put the panko and put the covered artichokes and shake until coated.

Put the prepared artichokes in Air Fryer and cook at the maximum temperature of around 10-15 mins.

For any leftover artichokes, extract & repeat.

Sprinkle with cheese and parsley.

Serve with sauce right away if needed.

Nutrients:

Amount per serving

Calories: 110kcal

Carbs: 5g

Fat: 7g

Protein: 3g

6.37 Ranch Seasoned Air Fryer Chickpeas:

Cooking time: 22 minutes

Servings: 8

Ingredients:

- 1 15 oz only drained chickpeas
- 4 tsp dried dill
- 1 tbsp olive oil
- 2 tsp garlic powder
- ¾ tsp sea salt
- 2 tsp onion powder
- 1 tbsp lemon juice

Instructions:

Toss together chickpeas with 1 tbsp of liquid you have retained from the can in the small cup. Fry for 12 minutes at 400 °F.

Return the chickpeas to a small bowl and toss them with dill, olive oil, onion powder, garlic powder, lemon juice & salt so that the beans are neatly covered.

Switch chickpeas again to the air fryer container then cook for another 5 minutes at 350° F.

Serve now or fully cool and put in an airtight jar afterward.

Nutrients:

Amount per serving

Calories: 90kcal

Carbs: 3g

Fat: 2g

Protein: 4g

Chapter 07: 30 Day Meal Plan

To make it easy for you what sort of recipe you should have, we have made an outline of 30 days meal plan so that, you could have an idea of how to include a healthy diet and meals in your daily routine. And with the wide variety of recipes, you can easily switch the recipes that are the best alternate for you as per your preference and liking.

7.1 Week 1

1. Seafood Tacos
2. Air Fried Southwest-Style Pork Loin
3. Air Fryer Paprika Chicken Wings
4. Wedged Potatoes
5. Meatball Pasta Bake
6. Spicy Buttermilk Fried Chicken with Pepper Jelly Drizzle
7. BBQ Pulled Pork-Stuffed Corn Muffins
8. Rosemary and Salt Roasted Shrimp with Garlic Butter Dipping Sauce
9. Crispy Air-Fried Shrimp Sliders
10. Air Fried French toast
11. Snapper Fillets Baked in a Creole Sauce
12. Rotisserie Chicken
13. Air Fried Cinnamon Rolls
14. Buttermilk Fried Chicken
15. Southwest Cowboy Steak with Skillet Corn Sauce and Tortillas
16. Air Fried Bagels
17. Asian Air Fried Flounder
18. Crab Meat Imperial
19. Dehydrated Strawberries in the Power Air Fryer 360
20. Flank Steak
21. Giant Stuffed Burger

7.2 Week 2

1. Sunday Roast Beef with Gravy
2. Brown Butter-Pecan Bread Pudding with Bourbon Sauce
3. Sicilian-Style Air Fried Broccoli
4. Baby Bam Burgers
5. Cinco Leches Cake
6. Blue Cheese-Stuffed Burgers
7. Pecan-Crusted Codfish
8. White Chocolate Macadamia Bread Pudding
9. Mac & Cheese
10. Spicy Short Ribs Smothered with Red Gravy

11. Lemon Poppyseed Cake

12. Baked Mushrooms Stuffed With Crabmeat Imperial

13. Roasted Leg of Lamb

14. Air Fried Peanut Butter and Jelly Doughnuts

15. Gougeres Stuffed with Ham Mousse

16. Cornish Hens

17. Air Fried Buttermilk Biscuits

18. Garlicky Air Fried Shrimp

19. Emeril's Stuffed Shrimp

20. Scallion and Cheddar Biscuits

21. Fried Green Beans with Garlic Lime Dip

7.3 Week 3

1. Bacon and Corn Pudding

2. New York-Style Thin Crust Pizza

3. Korean Beef Wraps

4. Steak Roulade

5. Reuben Sandwich

6. Wild Mushroom and Manchego Pizza

7. Roasted Garlic White Pizza with Garlic Sauce

8. Roasted Salmon

9. Mini Pizzas with Hot Italian Sausage

10. Pecan Crusted Chicken

11. Blue Cheese-Stuffed Burgers

12. Bourbon Rotisserie Pork Roast

13. Kicked-Up Tuna Melts

14. Shrimp & Pork Vietnamese Egg Rolls

15. Air Fried Frozen Biscuit and Sausage Patty

16. Air Fried Citrus and Honey Glazed Ham

17. Bacon Wrapped Asparagus

18. Air Fried New York Strip Steak with Red Wine Sauce

19. Garlicky Air Fried Shrimp

20. Air Fried Roasted Duck

21. Air Fried Crispy Brussels sprouts with Lemon, Garlic, and Parmesan

7.4 Week 4

1. Air Fryer Cherry Turnovers

2. Air Fried Garlic Bread

3. Air Fried Wontons

4. Air Fried Bacon

5. Sweet Potato Pie in an Air Fryer

6. Air Fried Tater Tots

7. Air Fried Frittata

8. Air Fryer Strawberry Pop-Tarts

9. Air Fried Cheese Stuffed Mushrooms

10. Air Fried Egg and Bacon Bite Cups

11. Air Fryer Dessert Empanadas

12. Air Fried Potato Wedges

13. Air Fried Sausage

14. Air Fried Mini Corn dogs

15. Air Fried Cheesy Garlic Bread

16. Air Fried French toast Sticks

17. Grilled Chicken Breast Strips

18. Air Fried Crunchy Pickles

19. Air Fried Blueberry Muffins

20. Air Fried Cornbread

21. Crispy Air Fried Sweet Potato Hash Browns

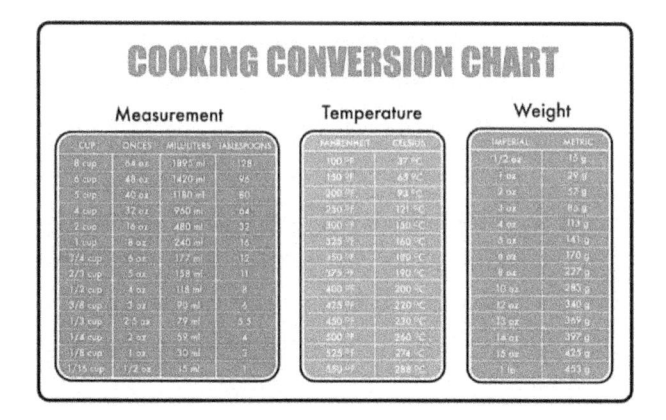

Conclusion:

Replace your convection oven with an air fryer from Lagasse. For perfect, smooth cooking, five of the heating components replicate an oven of industrial quality. The majority of convection ovens have just 3. You can pick whether you want to prepare and how to set 12 already set features for cooking, custom oven setting for toaster for up to 6 slices of bread, roast a whole turkey, bake cakes, air fry the chicken, roast the veggies, slow cooking process for up to ten hours, bake pizza, dehydrate berries and jerky, and more. Better than regular convection ovens, rapid 360° cooking design and five strong heating components ensure that your meals cook equally on all sides and make moist, delicious tastes in a swirl of much heated air. No added oils, fats, or harmful fats are required. Get some professional of results in a lightweight countertop oven with 1500 of the watts and 40% quicker than standard ovens. It will help you minimize the amount of unnecessary calories you eat by up to 70 percent by choosing an air fryer over a conventional fryer used for deep frying while also making you enjoy your favorite and delicious foods.

About all that you can think of this can prepare. You can conveniently make bagels, chicken, chicken tender or steak, pizza, anything breaded, and much more if you search for its preset options. It's also significant to note that the temperature and time can be adjusted manually. If your meal is too cold or hot for a preset moment, then ditch its preset and make some changes using the temperature knobs. There are several accessories needed for the best air fryer. This makes the fryer easier to use, and also to make your fryer actually useful, as it prevents you from needing to purchase trays, pans, etc. Therefore, the accessory kit contains the baking pan, Rotisserie Spit, Crisper Tray, Drip Tray and Pizza Rack. Not only that, but can also place the accessories in several positions, meaning you can use both the baking pan and the crisper tray at the same time to complete your meal easily. Whenever practicable, we recommend using the drip tray to catch drippings and fat. When you are done, it helps your cleaning process even easier.

CPSIA information can be obtained
at www.ICGtesting.com
Printed in the USA
BVHW011814080922
646576BV00011B/207